LIFE-CHANGING MIRACLES

Books Compiled and Written by James Stuart Bell

From Bethany House Publishers

Life-Changing Miracles

Gifts From Heaven

Jesus Talked to Me Today

Encountering Jesus

Heaven Touching Earth

The Spiritual World of the Hobbit

Angels, Miracles, and Heavenly Encounters

From the Library of A.W. Tozer

From the Library of Charles Spurgeon

Love Is a Flame

Love Is a Verb (with Gary Chapman)

Love Is a Verb Devotional (with Gary Chapman)

LIFE-CHANGING MIRACLES

Real-Life Stories *of* Unforgettable
Encounters *with* God

COMPILED BY
JAMES STUART BELL

BETHANYHOUSE
a division of Baker Publishing Group
Minneapolis, Minnesota

In keeping with biblical principles of creation stewardship, Baker Publishing Group advocates the responsible use of our natural resources. As a member of the Green Press Initiative, our company uses recycled paper when possible. The text paper of this book is composed in part of post-consumer waste.

green
press
INITIATIVE

To Mike McAlister—
may Jesus change your life today,
tomorrow,
and forever.

God has given to man a short time here upon earth, and yet upon this short time eternity depends.

Jeremy Taylor (1613–1677)

Contents

Contents

Contents

Contents

Acknowledgments

I'm in debt to my ever faithful editor, Andy McGuire, along with Ellen Chalifoux, Amanda Clawson, Julie Smith, Miranda Eiden, Stacey Theesfield, Chandler Carlson, Grace Kasper, Patnacia Goodman, Shaun Tabatt, and Robin Turici.

Introduction

Some events in our lives are so overwhelming and so powerful that we know almost immediately they will change our lives from that point forward—the way we think, the way we act, the way we view God or the world. And as we move on in life's journey, there are still other events that at the time may seem insignificant but have a subtle yet profound influence on us over the years.

In fact, we realize in both cases that there was an element of the miraculous involved that displayed God's involvement, especially as we look at the effects on our lives. Thus, the title of this book of personal stories: *Life-Changing Miracles*. All it takes for a miracle is God's involvement that goes beyond human abilities. And all it takes for our lives to be changed is His continual grace and power in light of that divine involvement over the ensuing years.

Miracles can be either dramatic or subtle, and so can the results in our lives. But to whatever degree these stories reflect a supernatural experience of God's presence and power, they demonstrate His extraordinary work in our lives. These events are not easily forgotten and have an impact going forward in terms of the kind of person we are and who we will become. Yes, at times the process may even be difficult, but God's primary purpose is to change our lives. His goal in sanctification is to change us from sinners in bondage to death into sons and daughters of God having the eternal life of Christ, being glorified in freedom in His image.

It is my hope that as you read these stories, you, too, will better envision the miracles—whether big or small—in your own life, and be changed by reading of God's supernatural work in the lives of these contributors.

James Stuart Bell

Truck Driver Betty

PATTI ANN THOMPSON

S he was hard to miss when you entered the room. Truck Driver Betty stood six-feet-plus in military tennis shoes with the shoulders and arms of a lumberjack.

She was easily the size of two of me, although no one would call her chubby. Stocky would be a better choice of words if you wanted to see the light of another day!

Those who had the courage to look closer saw a leathered face reflecting her years on the road. Her occasional smile was hidden among rolls of wrinkles. Bleached blond hair neatly tied back in a ponytail, faded blue jeans, and a paisley blouse finished her look.

Betty sat in the first chair of the first row in the first group of the assembly stations. An appropriate position considering she ruled the 3–11 night shift—if not in title, certainly in personage!

I nodded and smiled at her as I passed by on my way to my newest home away from home. It was my first night on the job at our local automotive parts plant. Both my teenage sons were now in high school, and the financial demands made it necessary for me to step out of my comfort zone and enter the work world. Fortunately for me, the 3 to 11 shift was made up of mostly women; many had similar stories to mine.

"Patti Ann, do you want to join us on break?" a friendly voice over my shoulder inquired. Carol sat directly behind me, and the invitation to join anyone on my first night was a welcomed gift. I was learning to solder tiny wires together in car parts, and boy, could I use an "Aw, it'll get better" conversation!

"Thanks, I'm more than ready," I answered as I rose to follow her to the break room.

With drinks in hand we made our way to a table to rest, a table that already included Truck Driver Betty. Apparently Carol was the only friend Betty had. She slid into the vacant chair next to Betty, a chair that I would learn always seemed conveniently empty.

"Patti Ann, this is my friend Betty. She was a truck driver for many years before retiring and coming here to work." I later learned she had been married for many years, and her husband had deserted her.

Betty never raised her eyes or spoke, content to stare intently at her own drink. Carol introduced the other members at the table, fellow workers full of questions about the new gal on the block.

It didn't take long for them to learn about my life in Christ. Nightly, I received opportunities to share stories of answered prayer from my life and others' lives. Nightly, the curious listeners began opening up and telling their own stories. Each of us on the night shift received a special nickname assigned by the group—mine was Pastor Pat.

Betty never joined our conversations. She sometimes watched me intently as I shared, but mostly she just stared at her drink as if she couldn't care less about the conversations that took place. Until one night . . .

"Gals, this is Julie," Carol's friendly voice boomed to those at our table. "She is filling in for Debbie. She'll only be with us for one night."

It didn't take Julie long to make her mark on the group. She immediately began telling an off-color joke and used several swear words in her dialogue.

"Don't ever use that kind of language at this table again! We have a pastor sitting at this table!"

Startled, we turned our heads. For the first time in the few weeks I had been there, Truck Driver Betty had spoken! And when Betty spoke, everybody listened!

She shot a look in my direction, smiled, and returned to her fixation on her drink. An unspeakable bond formed that night between Betty and me. I began to pray that God would somehow touch her life and let her know personally how much He loved her. It was an impossible task for others to reach her, but God could find a way.

A few days later, I was late getting to the break room.

"Patti Ann, Betty is looking for you," Carol reported as she brushed by me.

What? Betty, looking for me?

I had just finished paying for my drink when Betty came around the corner, literally dragging an older man with her.

"Pastor Pat, this man's son was diagnosed with a heart problem today and is facing triple bypass surgery," she said sternly.

"I told him I knew someone who knew God and would pray for him."

With that said, she handed the man off to me and went back to her table.

What is the greater miracle here? I wondered at my station later. *Is it the fact that Betty spoke to me, or the incredible gesture of reaching out to someone in need? All those times she was sitting, listening to our conversations about how God answers prayer. Is God chipping away at her heart, one testimony at a time? Has He been drawing her to himself and I've missed it?*

I began that day to pray more earnestly than before for God to touch her life personally.

That was not the last time Betty brought others to me for prayer. Though she never requested prayer for herself, she seemed to find other needy souls to bring for prayer and a word about God.

Before long, some unexpected events in my life meant I had to leave my evening job and my new friends. By this time, I had an intense desire to see Betty come to know God's love for herself. I asked God to give me the opportunity to share with her one-on-one, something she had avoided during the entire time I was there.

My last night arrived. We had two breaks each night, so I hoped I could talk personally to Betty at one of them. At first break everyone wanted to say their good-byes, and the time passed quickly. Betty, unusually quiet and aloof that night, neither looked at nor spoke to anyone. The second break time came, and I waited for Betty at the entry to the break room.

"Is Betty coming?" I asked when Carol came into the break room.

"No, she's not feeling well tonight and has a migraine head-ache," Carol answered empathetically. "She is in a lot of pain but doesn't want to go home. I think she is lying down on her break."

That was it then. No chance to talk to her before I left. I would never see her again. Again a prayer for Betty. *Please, God, let her know you love her, too.*

I saw Betty return a little while later to her first chair in the first row in the first group. Though my seat was two sections behind hers, I could see Betty's figure towering far above the stack of soldered plates at my station.

Then I heard it: *Go to Betty and lay your hands on her head and pray for her.*

I dismissed the thought as my own sincere desire and con-tinued to work.

Go to Betty and lay your hands on her head and pray for her.

Again the prompting came, this time more intense. I began to believe that this could be God's direction and threw out an outlandish test to find out.

"God, if that is you speaking to me, when I look around my stack of car parts, Betty will be holding her head in her hands."

I waited a few moments, somewhat anxious about the pros-pect of laying hands on Betty for any reason. Finally, I found the courage to look around the stack of car parts toward Betty.

Betty was sitting still, holding her head in her hands.

Without hesitation—and I'm sure with courage from God—I walked to Betty's station. Betty looked up at me.

With a quivering voice I said, "Betty, God sent me here to lay hands on your head and to pray for your headache to be healed."

She sat motionless. I prayed and quickly retreated to my seat.

Now it was I who sat motionless, my heart racing, my eyes fixated on the object in front of me. I guess I didn't notice when she arrived next to me. But my downward gaze recognized the all-too-familiar military tennis shoes. They were Betty's.

I raised my face slowly until our eyes met. Tears were streaming down her cheeks, and for the first time I saw burly Truck Driver Betty shake with emotion.

"My headache is gone," she said. "I don't understand it, but all the pain is gone!"

"Oh, dear Betty," I replied, barely able to say the words through my own tears. "God has touched you. He has healed you. He did it so you would know how much He loves you."

God had indeed answered prayer. Betty came to know Him personally that night. I heard later that Betty was still in charge of the night shift, but now God was using her to pray for others. And the others at the break table had given her a new nickname: Merciful Betty.

Persistence in Healing

RICHARD SPILLMAN

W e all remember the firsts in our lives. They always mark a transition of some sort. Your first car lingers in your memory as the gateway to a newfound freedom. Your first home is the sign of a newfound responsibility. But for me, the first time God used me to heal a friend marked a different kind of transition: a transition into a new relationship with the Father.

It took a long time for my first healing experience to occur, but when it came I was more than ready for the transition. For more than twenty years I prayed for others to be healed. Usually they were tentative prayers asking God to direct the doctors to heal a loved one. There is nothing wrong with praying for our doctors; they need wisdom to do their work. But I always felt there was more that I should be doing when I entered the presence of God in prayer.

I eventually reached the point where I was so hungry for a healing experience that I decided it was time for boldness. Tentative, even timid, prayers would have to go. Jesus gave the apostles the command to heal the sick (Matthew 10:7–8) and also sent out the seventy-two disciples with a similar command: "Heal the sick, and tell them, 'The Kingdom of God is near you now'" (Luke 10:9). He didn't say to go out and ask God to heal the sick; the command is quite clear. It was their responsibility to let Jesus heal through them. It was now time for me to boldly proclaim healing in the name of Jesus.

I wish I could say that the first time I prayed in this manner someone was healed, but it didn't happen that way. Yet I was not about to be discouraged. I was going to go after healing with the same persistence with which the widow of the parable went after the judge (Luke 18:1–8).

It happened quite unexpectedly one cold Sunday morning after church. I am the associate pastor of the Downtown Crossing, a church for the homeless in Tacoma, Washington. After the service, a homeless woman named Ann got up from her seat and struggled to move to the front. She grimaced in obvious pain as she used the chairs for support. She asked our pastor, Ben, for prayer, explaining that she had a very painful attack of gout and could barely walk. Ben had to help a person in a wheelchair get down stairs, so he asked another woman nearby, Matilda, and me if we would pray for her.

Matilda and I placed our hands on Ann's shoulder. We commanded the pain to leave in the name of Jesus. We commanded her legs to heal. All of a sudden, Ann let out a cry, "Whoa, what was that?" Neither Matilda nor I had noticed anything; we had barely started praying. I asked Ann what happened. Ann said she felt warmth spread down from the top of her head to the bottom of her feet. She suddenly felt at peace. I asked her how her legs felt. She paused to think for a moment about my question. Her attention had focused so much on the calming warmth that had engulfed her body that she hadn't thought about the pain at all. Now she realized that it was gone. She told me that all the pain in her left leg was completely gone and her right leg was just a little uncomfortable.

While she did not leap on her way out of the room, she did walk at a normal pace without requiring the help of the chairs. As Ben met her, he noticed that she was crying. Not knowing what had just happened, he asked, "Why the tears?" Her answer was remarkable. She was not crying because she had been healed; rather, she told Ben that she had "just been touched by God."

This was the first time I had prayed for someone and they had been instantly healed. It was Ann's time to be touched by God, and it was my moment of transition. I had learned a lot during my long struggle to see God heal. I had learned the power of boldness and the virtue of persistence. Most of all, I learned the power of faith. I knew that God wanted to heal, that He had the power to heal, and I was not going to let those times when healing did not occur change that belief. Every time I prayed and there was no healing, I became more determined than ever to seek healing the next time I prayed. I knew all along that one day I would meet someone like Ann and that I would see a miracle. Now that day had come and I would never be the same again.

Ann was not the only one healed that day. My life was changed, as well. Since that day I have continued to pray just as boldly as I did with Ann. Not everyone I have prayed for has been healed, but some have. I prayed and saw a woman's left leg grow to the length of her right leg. I prayed for a deaf ear to be opened and shared in the joy when a woman heard sounds for the first time. I saw God heal a lifetime of back pain as I prayed. But I will never forget the first time I saw God heal. The image of Ann walking away fully restored, proclaiming through her tears that she had been touched by God, is forever burned into my memory.

So, like me, if you have not seen God heal, be bold, be persistent, because there is a first time coming in your future, as well. Someday you will meet and pray for someone just like Ann. Someday you will have a new first in your life.

Ride of a Lifetime

DIANNE FRASER

The clouds hung heavy with snow over the glacier, and to five-year-old Jayden it meant his dreams of a helicopter ride were over. We'd planned our trip to New Zealand from our home in Australia for the past year, and each of us had chosen one thing we would love to do. Jayden's first flight in a chopper was his choice, and it was something we had all eagerly anticipated.

The tour operator called to confirm that we would not be flying in the morning. In the grand scheme of things, it was not the end of the world, but it seemed like it to our young son.

In an effort to explore all the possibilities, we scanned the weather forecast for the coming days and spoke to the tour operators and even the locals, who all shook their heads at a change in prospects. It all pointed the same way: We may as well pack up the camper van and head on. New Zealand weather had set in, and an anticipated highlight of our holiday was looking like a non-event.

As we tucked Jayden into bed that night, we tried to placate him with new suggestions and other opportunities and adventures that lay ahead in the coming days.

"We could go jet-boating, and Puzzling World looks fantastic." As we tumbled over ourselves to help him navigate his disappointment, he looked calmly out at us and declared, "No, we will go for a helicopter ride tomorrow morning."

Seeking to suppress our frustration, we told him again that this would not happen.

"They aren't flying tomorrow, Jayden. The tours can't run if the weather is poor."

"Well, I asked God to take away the clouds in the morning," he said, looking up at us from his pillow. "God heard me ask."

My heart sank. If it wasn't enough to deal with his holiday disappointment, we would also have to deal with damage to his budding faith when God didn't come through.

"Well, sometimes God knows what's best for us, and maybe He thinks it is better if we do something different," I said. Trying to think of all the platitudes and reasons why God wouldn't change an entire weather forecast for a five-year-old, I let him fall asleep with his hopes and went for a walk.

"What am I supposed to tell him, God? He's just starting to believe that you care for him, and I don't know that his young heart will understand. How do I tell him that what we want doesn't always happen, even when we pray?" I questioned.

As I walked around the tourist park under heavy skies, I spent a significant amount of time and energy wondering how I would defend God's position, as God clearly would not act on such an inconsequential prayer.

We fell asleep in our temporary home while considering the logistics of where we would head to the following day.

"Mum, Mum," a little voice whispered into my dreams. "Mum, the sun is shining." My husband rolled over and grunted, "We just need a little more sleep, Jayden."

"But you need to tell the helicopter man we need tickets."

My eyes popped open, and sure enough, sunshine was creeping through the curtains.

We both bolted upright, trying to push aside the sleep enough to discover if this was a dream or reality.

Not only was the sun bright and clear, but no clouds marred the view of the mountain, and the air was still and calm.

"What on earth . . . ?"

"God heard me ask Him to make the sky clear, so He did," our five-year-old stated factually.

My husband and I looked at each other with surprise. We called the tour operator as soon as we could and were scheduled to fly within the hour.

The ride was magical. Deep crevices within the glacier were wondrous to see. As we gazed through the glass nose of the helicopter, we watched the majesty of God's creation pass beneath us. Jayden sat next to the pilot. Wonder filled his face and his smile melted my heart. His little brother, Callum, sat on my lap, also mesmerized.

We landed on the summit and had time to step into the unbroken snow.

"God heard me, Mum. I knew He would," he said as he threw a snowball at me. The wonder of the scenery, the majesty of being on the top of a mountain, the pristine beauty of glaringly fresh snow were nothing short of brilliant, but God's presence in that moment resonated with me so intensely that I wanted to cry.

We returned to the base of the mountain just as fresh clouds started to roll in and the tour company put up a sign: "Closed due to bad weather." God had opened up the opportunity of a lifetime for a five-year-old boy.

That day taught me a lot. God does care about the desires of our hearts—even those of a child. The concerns don't have to be life altering. Sometimes God just delights in being able to provide us with joy.

I learned not to assume I know God's heart and not to express doubt about how others are trusting in Him.

God does hear. He does do the miraculous. And a child's belief in a loving Father reminded me of that truth.

Roid Rage!

SUSAN ERYK

Have you ever heard of roid rage? It's when a body builder on steroids loses control and starts throwing things and hurting people. It's terrifying! My husband and I have seen it in the flesh.

We were raising three kids—two teenagers and one preteen. Our daughter was the oldest. She didn't get into much trouble, but when she did, it was a pretty big deal. When she broke curfew, we decided to ground her.

When her dad told her this, she didn't like it, but surprisingly went to her room without too much lip. That should have made us suspicious, because she was usually pretty vocal, but it was an hour or so before I started to question why Jenn's room was inexplicably quiet.

I peeked in. Jenn wasn't there. I realized she must have slipped out through her bedroom window and called her friend Lisa to pick her up. As I looked around the room, I realized Jennifer wasn't the only thing that was missing.

We called the police right away. We gave them Lisa's address and the description of her car. When the dispatcher asked me how I knew our daughter was a runaway and not just hanging out with her friend, I told them about her most prized possession—her beautiful custom-made performance saber—not being in its place in her room. Jenn was in color guard, and her saber was her vital piece of equipment. She could have run away without taking her clothes, but she would never have left that saber behind.

Finding Jenn was easy enough, but getting her to come back with us was traumatic.

The police officer had suggested that we go to Lisa's house and politely request that they not harbor a fugitive. When we got there, we found her mother and older brother, Billy, were also home. They seemed quite cordial and invited us in. We sat on the couch, politely discussing our concerns, when Lisa's brother, a huge body builder with massive muscles, started literally throwing furniture around. He asked us to step outside. For some stupid reason, I thought we'd be safer outside, where there were no coffee tables for him to throw, but we soon learned there was no safe place to talk to Billy.

He went into a full roid rage and started punching my husband in the face. I screamed and tried to push this hulk away from my husband—unsuccessfully, of course.

"Leave him alone! He just had eye surgery!" I cried, trying to appeal to the human side of Big Billy. Instantly I realized my mistake: He didn't have a human side. He knocked my husband to the ground and kept kicking him.

Finally, by some miracle, Billy's mother got him to stop. One more minute of that beating and I would have passed out for sure. But worse, my husband would have been dead!

When the whole nasty thing was over, Jennifer sided with her dad's attacker instead of with her dad, who, in that moment, seemed that he would die for her.

I almost lost my mind that night. I had never been so close to mental collapse. I kept saying to my husband, "I'm sorry. This is my fault. I almost got you killed."

Never once did he say, "That was Billy's fault. How was that your fault?"

When we got home, I went to my room and screamed into my pillow until I couldn't scream any more. What must my poor children have thought? Unfortunately, I wasn't thinking of them at that moment. I wasn't my normal self. I was a lunatic! I just kept screaming into my pillow. I begged God to kill me. Fortunately, He had other ideas.

With all of my carrying on, I almost failed to see God's miracle. When my crying and screaming settled to sobbing and whimpering, my husband looked down at his T-shirt and said to me, "What just happened? Why is my shirt all crushed like this? It looks like someone grabbed my shirt and twisted it into a ball. And why am I so dirty?"

I looked at him in sheer disbelief.

"What are you talking about? That guy just basically beat the stuffing out of you. Don't you remember?"

"I knew he was really mad," Mike said. "I could hear him screaming. I didn't feel anything, though. He didn't hurt me."

Mike lifted his T-shirt. Sure enough, he didn't have a mark on his body. Keep in mind, the guy who tried to kick him to death was at least thirty pounds heavier, and he was all muscle and fury! God had protected Mike that night. Some poor guardian angel was probably pretty bruised up!

God had protected me, too. In trying to push the ogre away from my husband, I sustained muscle damage. I'm only five feet two, and when I think of how big the guy was, I know my injuries could have been much worse.

The greatest damage of all, though, was to my emotional state. It took me a long time to recover emotionally from that night.

Two things were crystal clear to me, though. First of all, I knew God wasn't finished with my husband or me just yet. He certainly had His chance to take either of us, or both of us, out that night, but He didn't.

I also learned that God is *way* more powerful than some body builder on steroids. And He's got my back.

Something about facing death makes you reevaluate things. I prayed for myself to be a better parent. I asked God to show me my shortcomings, and over time, He did.

But my husband and I also parented with more confidence than before. Romans 8:31 points out that if God is for us, who can be against us? I prayed for my kids more because I realized God was supernaturally partnering with my husband and me to raise our kids. We didn't have to go it alone; we could have God's help.

The kids are grown now. Both of our sons are living for the Lord. They married women who are beautiful on the inside and out, who also love the Lord.

As for Jennifer, my husband and I are still waiting for God to do another miracle in her life—the biggest miracle of all. We're waiting for her to finally submit to Christ and live for Him. Until then, my husband and I will keep praying because we know God has our backs. He's bigger than some body builder on steroids. He's bigger than any mistakes my husband and I made when we were raising our kids. He's bigger than anything that could possibly stand in the way of our daughter's eventual salvation. Hallelujah! He's bigger than anything!

A Walking Miracle

JULIE MILLER

I was all grown up, or so I thought. I had my own apartment. I had a great job at a law firm downtown. Life was more than I could've dreamed it to be.

As I walked to my car that warm August Friday night after a week's worth of work, I counted myself blessed.

I rolled down my windows, turned the radio on, and with a song in my heart, wound my way back toward the suburbs. But my apartment wasn't my final destination. I was hitting the road for a little weekend trip to help my brother celebrate his eighth birthday.

After a quick change into a tank top, shorts, and flip-flops, I grabbed his gift, my backpack, and away I went.

I had traveled this length of freeway many times. I could've almost driven it blindfolded. As the wind swept in through my open window, I thought of my boyfriend and his buddies standing in line at the theater to see *Star Wars*. I would've liked to have joined them, but my little brother was more than precious to me, and I wouldn't have missed his party for the world.

When I was nearly halfway to my destination, the steering wheel jerked hard to the left, veering my car toward the ditch. I tried to steer the car back right, but my front left tire had hit the gravel along the shoulder of the road. Then my car spun, facing oncoming traffic. As I hit the gravel again, this time on the passenger side, the car flipped into the grassy median.

As the car rolled, everything seemed to move in slow motion. I saw the windshield shatter, its shards coming at me. I felt myself floating upward . . . only I was upside down. My head banged against the roof. Without a seat belt, I was tossed in a heap against the passenger door just as the car came to rest on its wheels once more.

I'd seen far too many movies with cars blowing up, so the only thought in my jumbled head was of escaping. I heaved the door open with every ounce of strength I could muster and stepped out. Three young men were waiting there to catch me as I passed out.

The next thing I remember, I was lying on my back in the grass with grasshoppers playing hopscotch over me. Cars lined the freeway like a parking lot. Folks encircled me. My mind whirled, my heart raced, but my lips were silent.

I was unconscious when they placed me in the ambulance, but awoke to the bright hospital lights and a semicircle of doctors and nurses around me. I still couldn't speak a word. I could only point to where it hurt.

They rushed me to the X-ray unit.

My neck ached with every movement. I wept silently each time they positioned me on the table. I could only pray for God's mercy to hold me.

I was then wheeled back to the ER and placed in a curtained-off cubicle to await results. My mom and stepdad arrived shortly after that, only to be told I was being released. The doctor said I had only suffered whiplash.

The car ride back to my apartment was painful. Even with a collar on for support, my neck ached with every bump.

The next day I awoke with a horrible headache. But with a steady stream of visitors, I wasn't able to lie down until after suppertime. Exhausted, I asked my roommate, Rhonda, and my boyfriend, Rey, to help me into bed.

Ever so carefully they cupped my head and back and began to lower me. But still, something slipped in my neck and suddenly I couldn't breathe. I panicked and immediately stood to my feet, trying to catch my breath.

Rhonda called the hospital, and Rey and I rushed back to the emergency room. Every little jostle was painful. But somehow the jostling had helped me start breathing again.

A while after I arrived at the hospital, a doctor said he'd looked at my X-rays and that nothing was wrong with my neck, that whiplash can be painful, and the pain can last for several months. He gave me a muscle relaxant and sent me home with the following advice: "Quit being such a baby."

So I went back to work.

But over the next three months my body deteriorated. I felt like I was walking ten inches off the ground. My bladder became unpredictable; I'd run to the bathroom with urgency, only to be unable to empty. Then I'd empty without any warning.

My boss, whom I adored, called me into his office one day and said that he had grown concerned. He had noticed that my work had gotten sloppy and that I often seemed confused, not at all like the Julie he had known before. And my co-workers were also concerned.

I broke down and cried. I said, "I didn't realize I was making mistakes. Please don't let me go. I love this job!"

He said he had no intention of letting me go. He just wanted me to see a doctor.

I didn't have a family doctor, so I went to my family chiropractor.

Dr. Abeler sat me down in his office the following day and asked me to explain some of my symptoms. As I shared, he shook his head and made notes. I felt sure he was going to tell me to go home and quit acting like a baby. But instead he took X-rays, told me to drive home carefully, and said he'd get back to me after he read the X-rays.

Early the next morning the phone rang. Dr. Abeler said that I needed to get to the hospital immediately and that he would have the X-rays sent there.

"Do you have someone to take you?" he asked. "If not, drive as carefully as possible, please, because I think I found a fracture in your neck."

The hospital was abuzz when I arrived. I was put flat on my back on a gurney and was told a neurosurgeon would come to talk to me. They placed a phone on my chest and asked me to call someone to be there with me when the doctor spoke to me. I called my dad.

The neurosurgeon, Dr. Martin, explained that my neck was broken between my first and second cervical vertebrae, and that most people who break their neck there don't live to talk about it. Also, the odontoid process, the little bony piece that holds it all together, had broken off and was floating in my spinal column.

"The area where your neck is broken is the operating system for your heart, lungs, bladder, etc.," he said. "That is why you were having a hard time breathing and why your bladder malfunctioned. One morning you could've turned in bed to hit your alarm and your neck would've severed your spinal cord, and you would've died. You are nothing short of a walking miracle! However, the surgery I'm going to be doing is dangerous. Just opening your neck up could potentially kill you. I give you about a 30 percent chance of living through it. But at this point, you really don't have an alternative."

And they say neurosurgeons have no bedside manner!

Remarkably, I had a supernatural sense of peace. I believed with all of my heart that God would heal me, be it an earthly healing or a heavenly one. If He had a plan for me here on earth, I would live out that plan to bless His heart. If not, I would live out His plan in my heavenly home.

A few days later, after Dr. Martin gathered my family around me to say our good-byes, I was wheeled to the surgical suite. Under anesthesia, I was hung facedown from straps from the ceiling and a rib was removed that would act as a splint—it would be wired to hold my vertebrae in place.

When I came out of surgery nine hours later, I was wheeled to recovery, then to my room. Sometime after midnight I awoke to pinpricks on my feet and legs and to my dad's smiling face inches from my own. *I was alive!*

I remained hospitalized for four weeks. It was a slow recovery process, but my grandfather, who was a minister and in an eclectic prayer group of priests and multi-denominational pastors from the area, had asked these prayer warriors to place me on their twenty-four-hour-a-day prayer lists at their churches. And boy, could I feel those prayers in action!

Those precious men even took time to stop by often to sit with me and pray with me. And by God's grace and covered in prayer, I grew strong enough to go live with my grandparents for the next month.

After six months in a brace from the tip of my head to my waist, I was finally able to begin living life again.

And I've lived that miracle out every day to the best of my ability to bless my Savior's heart.

Vision of a Heavenly Warrior

Susan M. Watkins

As a shiny new believer, I was swept up in the grandeur of God's palpable presence. Leaping about my Good Shepherd's pasture, I surveyed my new spiritual home. It was safe, and I was confident in my Herdsman's ability to care for me. His one hand carried a capable shepherd's hook, but the other held a sturdy rod. I couldn't help but wonder what a weapon was doing in such an idyllic locale. His staff kept me from scampering under the fence or guided me away from dangerous curiosities, but why the rod?

My query was answered eons before I posed it. God *knows* His flock. He likewise knows His enemy. The line drawn in heaven, the usurper and constituents promptly swept out, and the final nail hammered into the enemy's future by a Carpenter on Calvary. For now, God has the guilty on a leash.

Enjoying my Shepherd's care brought me to an intersection of learning. It was time to understand the rod's purpose. Growing up in a large metropolis offered conveniences; however, beside the pros are the complicated cons. Unfortunately, the con column held a storied criminal history for many inhabitants.

In the aftermath that followed, I learned pivotal lessons. Fear can quickly spiral into sin. Suggesting this bristles against the compassion within us, but fear's unchecked presence challenges God's sovereignty. Natural fear has purposeful design, protecting us in multilayered applications. However, feeding fear, bowing to its insatiable demands, and becoming crippled by it is precisely where sin creeps in. It blinded me, obscuring my view of God. Unwittingly feeding it caused growth, and its harvest was rebellion against heaven. Sin.

Raised in an entrepreneurial and industrious family, I had launched into my working career early. While attending high school, I maintained two part-time jobs. My schedule was crowded, but I balanced it and enjoyed its rewards.

One winter evening the test arrived. Since I was only sixteen years old, my mode of transportation was walking. As the Lord actively sanctified where my feet currently took me, I embarked on my daily ritual of walking home after school/work. The winter solstice made for an early sunset, and I knew the dangers nightfall brought. I quickened my step and approached a busy intersection. Just one block left before my key unlocked my home. A traffic light change forced me to wait on the corner. It was characteristically cold but quiet, as a new foot of snow had fallen on the existing foot beneath it. Though bundled and shivering, I still heard the crunching of snow as a car stopped alongside me. Fear engulfed me, and with my heart pounding in my ears, I looked over my shoulder as car doors slammed.

Five men emerged and walked toward me, clearly hunting for a victim. Their expressions promised I was to become a statistic. I prayed for protection. The leader shoved me, and I fell back into the deep snow. Instantly, four men each pinned a limb. The leader pressed my head down, and I saw the glint of a large knife right before its icy blade pressed across my throat. I thought one of the passing cars would stop to prevent my gang rape, but none did.

My 104 pounds were no match for five strapping young men. I struggled in vain while they shouted threats at my face and pressed the knife deeper into my skin. I screamed for God's deliverance. The leader mocked me, saying that God couldn't hear me, causing the others to laugh. One man unzipped his pants while another began to unzip mine.

I continued screaming for divine intervention, and suddenly all five were simultaneously pushed away from me and looked terrified. They scrambled, slipping in the snow, and jumped into their car.

The tires spun wildly, spewing dirty snow behind them as they fled. I zipped my pants, sat up, and tried to make sense of what happened. I ran home and fell into my concerned mother's arms.

Though just a babe in Christ and still basking in the afterglow of salvation, I had a new constant companion: fear. Not just any fear—gripping fear. No one could fault me, given what I'd survived, but it was now consuming me. I'd stepped away from trusting God's care to questioning His intentions. He became less powerful in my eyes, with perceived lapses in His attention.

Little by little, I stopped trusting God and moved back into self-sufficiency. I no longer felt protected by heaven, even though I'd been miraculously rescued. I entertained the idea that if God *was* God, then He could have prevented the entire assault. If

He *really* loved me, a knife wouldn't have pressed against my throat while I was lying spread-eagle with people watching my attack. I started to harden. It was imperceptible at first, but the seeds sprouted roots.

I still had school and jobs requiring me to walk past the place of my attack twice daily. Tormenting fear complicated my new anger. I both loved and distrusted God, making me utterly miserable.

God is patient. He's so willing to be misunderstood. The Holy Spirit gently teaches with incomprehensible love. Each night I fell to my knees, crying angry, confused tears, trying to understand the One who will take eternity to comprehend. I'd somehow come to falsely believe nothing bad happens to Christians.

As sure as the earth revolves, seasons change. Winter gave way to spring, then summer. But I was still crippled with silent, terrifying fear. My daily walks to school and work were horrific. I knew He was with me but had abandoned the idea of His constant oversight. I was in the precarious position of straddling the fence. One foot was slung over to God's side and the other "worshiping" fear's side. You cannot serve two masters. I was wholly miserable.

God orchestrated my breaking point. Despite my attempts to grow in new faith, I gave God an ultimatum. All sixteen years of me challenged God. I announced I couldn't stand another minute chained to fear's slavery. I *had* to know He would protect me to my life's end.

I worked longer that day, and by the time I closed the store, armed it against robbery, and headed home, the sun was setting. I quickened my step. The streetlights would be flickering on soon. My neighborhood enjoyed mature oak trees, but it made my path even darker. I panicked at every sound.

As I approached the largest oak on the block, suddenly an enormous man stepped out from behind it and stood directly in my path. I screamed, but no sound exited my mouth. As we looked directly into each other's eyes, I thought he'd certainly kill me.

He continued looking at me, never breaking our gaze. He had a square, clean-shaven jaw, chiseled nose and cheekbones, squared fingers and toes. Wavy hair to his shoulders parted down the center.

A very long sword was attached at his waist, and he wore a long cape. He was muscular and dressed in unearthly battle attire. He was very tall—ten feet with a three-foot shoulder span. His flowing garments were brilliantly white, and eyes of fire burned with love and protection.

This was a mighty warrior whose feet never touched earth. His sheathed sword stretched from above his waist to just above his sandaled feet. His clothing moved softly from a breeze I never felt. He shifted his massive shoulders, and feathers appeared from behind him.

I strained for a closer look, and he fanned out his wings. He was so glorious I nearly fell over backward. Their opening sounded similar to a fast-moving waterfall. The tops of them were three feet above his shoulders and two feet past the edge of each arm, traveling the entire length of his body with a gentle curve at the bottom.

The wings were not spread for flight, just down in a resting position. Their feathers were varied in length, size, and appearance, but most spectacular was *each* feather was autonomously alive; however, they'd immediately synchronize as a unit at his bidding.

As we gazed at each other, my fear forever evaporated in the presence of such compelling authority. I knew I had favor with God, for one couldn't stand before such power without it and live.

With eyes fastened to mine, his enormous right hand grasped the hand guard of his sword. As he slowly separated the weapon from its holder, a sound emanated and intensified. Simultaneously, he grew brighter the further the sword was unsheathed, and his feathers quickened as this power intensified.

The sound was nearly deafening, and I felt its reverberation throughout my body until physically moved. When the tip exited its sheath, full power released with even greater sound, and my warrior glowed white-hot head to toe. He drew his massive double-edged sword upright and centered its blade over his chest, between his eyes, with its tip continuing three feet above his head.

He was a mere speck of God's majesty, and I understood the purpose of his presence before me. Never uttering a word, he looked fiercely through loving eyes and communicated that he was assigned to protect me for life.

I somehow remained upright throughout our encounter, staring at him. There comes a time when standing is all that's required. I realized then that this commander had removed my five would-be rapists. Recalling their collective fear, I knew undoubtedly that he had revealed himself to them.

I recognized God's love in his eyes and never wanted him to leave, but he began to fade until his ethereal light and presence disappeared from earth's view.

Somehow collecting myself, I raced home to tell Mom. The flimsy altar I'd built at fear's feet was demolished. I permanently turned from fear's siren song. As I rested, broken before the Lord for my disbelief, sinfulness, and sorrow, God did what He does best and lavishly forgave me.

I refused to question God's motives or capability in caring for His sheep. Yes, His rod brings equal comfort as His staff. Carefully fashioned from a tree's root at the junction where a knot occurs naturally, it's polished smooth, becoming a formidable weapon with a large ball at its end. Quite effective when dealing with sheep stealers, it's the soothing symbol of His willing readiness to act while shepherding His flock.

God has faithfully proven that His protective canopy solidly covers me. Decades later, I need only look over my shoulder to confirm that goodness and mercy are following me.

An Appointment with Jesus

TRISH PROPSON

Listening to yet another sermon about God's unending grace, I drifted into the familiar comfort of self-protection. Outwardly I listened and nodded, releasing an occasional "Amen." Inwardly, I ran through plans for my son's birthday party later that afternoon. There I was, a forty-two-year-old mother of four who never fully understood God's promise of grace, facing the same battle again.

I had been a devoted Christ follower for over thirty years and could honestly say that the whole concept of unmerited favor with God escaped me. I learned to dismiss grace as not applying to someone like me. Every time a new book on grace came out, someone inevitably gave it to me, and it ended up on my shelf with a dozen other unopened books on the subject. The concept of a sovereign God who would want to have anything to do with a wretch like me eluded me.

The doubts enslaving my soul screamed at me. How could the stains of my twisted and perverted past be erased? How could I possibly matter to the God of the universe? Why would He care about saving my sinful soul? How could I be so important to Him that He would kill His own Son to save me? I accepted on faith that these things were true, of course, but never fully embraced that this applied to me personally. How could it?

I am a survivor of unspeakable horrors. Before I found my way to God at age twenty-five, I spent most of my waking hours enduring violent abuse, denying myself, believing I was responsible, and hiding my shame at the risk of anyone seeing the scars branded into my heart.

My parents were loners who had no contact with their parents or extended family. They had no outside relationships with friends, neighbors, or co-workers. As a child, I was alone and afraid most of the time.

My father was a violent and abusive tyrant, an atheist who hated God and Christians. I was forbidden to have contact with people who attended church.

Since nearly everyone went to church in the 1960s, I had no friends. I never saw a Bible and had no idea who Jesus was.

My mother was withdrawn, mentally unstable, and incapable of love—scorning any physical touch or display of emotion. The only physical contact I experienced as a child was punishment or sexual abuse. I was constantly reminded that I was worthless, damaged, and unloved.

My dad left when I was twelve. My mother immediately became an alcoholic. Finding myself fatherless and motherless almost overnight, I was left to raise my younger brother.

I turned tragedy into overachievement at school and work. I graduated from high school at age fifteen and worked two jobs to put myself through college, hoping that would somehow make my pitiful life matter.

I never realized the tragic life I lived was abnormal. I thought everyone felt lost, alone, and despised. Not until my teen years did I begin to realize how dark my life really was.

With no one to guide me, I stumbled into an immoral and dangerous lifestyle, being violently abused and assaulted by many men and women. I became a wandering drug addict, using the most available resource I had—my body—to survive. I pleased men in exchange for food and a place to lay my head at night.

I tried to hold it together while keeping a job and continuing college, but I watched others who lived such different lives from mine, always wondering what they had that I didn't.

After a near-fatal beating and a drug overdose at age twenty-two, I realized that something had to change. My roommate called herself a Christian. Even though I didn't know what that meant, she said she prayed for me constantly. She kept telling me God loved me.

Yeah, sure He does, a sinister voice whispered.

After suffering horrible abuse for three more years, I contemplated suicide. My friend asked if I realized that everything I had used to fill the emptiness in my heart had failed. She said only God could shine His light in the dark places, replacing the pain with love and the light of a gift she called grace.

I agreed to go to church with her. But as my father had taught me, I sat in the back pew and mocked these foolish Christians. But I went back. And I went back again and again. As the weeks went on, I began to see something I had never seen before. These people loved each other. They had relationships and families and friends. They shared a common bond in their faith in some guy named Jesus. God began to shine His light into my dark heart.

One Sunday morning, I went to the church desperately hungover without a shred of hope left. I took my usual place in the back row, but that morning something was different. I saw the people more clearly and heard the words for the first time. About halfway through the worship, the pastor stood up and stopped the musicians.

He proclaimed, "One of you has an appointment with Jesus today. He has been waiting for you such a long time, and today is the day to surrender to Him."

He looked right at me huddled miserably in the back row and extended his hand. "Won't you come? Won't you give your life to Christ?"

In an instant, I felt the Spirit of God shoot through the top of my head and drop me to my knees as I felt Jesus invade my heart. I heard a new voice as God himself reached into my heart and whispered, *It is me. I'm here. You never have to be alone again. I love you.*

I spilled a lifetime of tears on the floor of that little church. For the first time in my life, I felt love. I knew there was a chance for a broken, ruined woman like me. They called it grace. Hope illuminated my dead soul. The service in that small church stopped as I surrendered my life to Christ. He saved me. My life was transformed in an instant.

Years later, I was a sold-out Christ follower in full-time ministry, struggling through yet another sermon on grace. In spite of my radical transformation decades earlier on the floor of that tiny church, remnants of my shameful past stubbornly filled the deepest cracks of my wounded heart. Transformation, it seems, is a lifelong process.

I returned from church with the promise of grace pounding in my head. I deeply longed to surrender the last remnant of shame to God, to let Jesus claim sovereign ownership of every little piece of my past, to finally claim freedom.

I prepared for my teen son's birthday party, which would start in a few hours. I once again wrestled with the truth of the sermon that morning. *God* loves me. God *loves* me. God loves *me*. I whispered a prayer, "Lord, please help me trust your love for me. Shine your light into my dark places. Take what is left of my shame and help me fully experience your grace."

I pushed my deep yearnings aside, and we welcomed guests, grilled burgers, opened gifts, and ate cake. Jacked up on soda, sugar, and testosterone, the fourteen-year-old boys played laser tag among the trees on our wooded property.

I cleaned up the party and watched from afar as they set up teams, drew battle lines, and decided on rules of engagement. The young warriors somberly strapped shields to their chests and carefully selected weapons. With battle cries that would terrify any unsuspecting passersby, they vanished beyond the inky darkness of the tree line.

The boys scattered silently into the night, stealthily stalking their opponents. Striking from behind trees and under bushes, they peered through laser scopes with precision and "shot" their enemies with laser beams. The only indication of which players were winning and which were losing were the red lights on their chest shields that blinked on and off once they were "wounded." After three consecutive hits, the red light remained on, exposing the "dead" player in the darkness.

I continued my conversation with God as I stared out the picture window. *God, I know you are here. I know you love me. Make it real to me. Let me see.*

51

A now-familiar voice broke through my doubt and sorrow. Jesus whispered to me, *Look at the boys. Do you see the light? That is why I came. I came for you because only a bloodred sacrifice redeems disgrace. I took your place on the cross. I died for your sin, for your shame, for those scars you so expertly hide in the dark places of your heart. Your past is invisible to me. Don't you remember? I love you.*

As if in unison with God's voice, the red lights from the laser tag shields glowed red, penetrating and illuminating my heart. I saw the true light of grace for the first time.

God doesn't see me for who I am—a lost, pitiful, selfish woman. All of my futile striving and attempts to find peace from my past are invisible to Him. My Father in heaven only sees the light of Jesus in me.

For the first time in my four-plus decades on this earth, I understood the mysterious blessing called grace. The laser-tag game unfolding before me was a simple illustration of the unfathomable truth that had escaped my understanding for so long. I watched in wonder as my new realization played out in these overactive teen boys.

As I stared into the night, the boys were invisible to me. When they came near the lone light in the yard, I recognized them. I saw their faces, knew their names, and identified who they were. As soon as they retreated, they were completely invisible to me again. It was as if they did not exist. I knew they were there, of course, but to me they were completely hidden. Only when the red lights on their chests activated could I see them through the darkness.

Of course! That is what Jesus wanted me to see that night. In His gentle, loving way, He spoke directly to me, pointing my heart toward a beautiful and unmistakable picture of His grace.

When we trust God, fully believing in the death and resurrection of His Son, Jesus Christ, the people we once were die, becoming completely invisible to Him. Our wretched lives, our past sin, our feeble strivings, consuming pride, and vain attempts at self-preservation are invisible—absolutely and joyously invisible. We completely disappear from His view.

Only when the redeeming blood of Jesus covers us can He see us again. And in that moment when we choose to put on the blood of Christ, He immediately recognizes us as His beloved children. Instead of my sinful nature, God sees only the light of Jesus in my place. That light alone is what makes Him reach toward me, showering me with His unending love and gift of amazing grace.

I am so thankful for a God who loves me in spite of my past. I am thankful Jesus reminds me of His love, even when I forget, and the transformation He began all those years ago is still underway. I can finally embrace the blessing of God's grace that revealed itself when Jesus whispered and I finally saw the light.

The Belly of the Beast

MOLLY NOBLE BULL

I'm not blaming anyone for what happened.

I should have known better than to fall into the New Age trap. But after reading gobs of occult books and magazines, I found myself in the camp of the enemy. At the time, I didn't know that Leviathan was that evil sea creature mentioned in the Bible or that having anything to do with the devil was extremely dangerous.

Remember the childhood story of Pinocchio, the little wooden puppet who refused to do as his father said and ended up in the belly of a whale? Well, I am ashamed to say that I was once a puppet, too, and like Pinocchio, I was swallowed up by a beast, despite the fact that I was reared in a mainline denominational church.

My family was Episcopalian. Growing up, I attended church most Sundays unless I was sick—whether at eight o'clock communion or at the family worship service later on Sunday mornings. Still, I knew almost nothing about the Bible and certain Old Testament Scriptures warning against the occult, Scriptures starting in Deuteronomy 18:9.

I married Charlie Bull when I was twenty-one years old, and by the time I was thirty-three, we had two of our three sons. I was also teaching at a local public elementary school. Though I was never a part of any organized New Age group, I read their literature and actually tried some of the outrageous things suggested in the books.

I'd joined an occult book club, and as part of my membership in the organization, I was given a crystal ball at the end of a gold chain and encouraged to use it. I would take hold of the end of the chain attached to the tiny crystal ball and ask the *thing* questions.

This sounds crazy to me now. But back then I was still reading books on the New Age Movement or what some might call idolatry literature. No, I didn't kneel down and worship graven images. However, I was deceived when I honored a tiny crystal ball by giving it respect and power that should have been reserved for God alone.

Yet all that changed one memorable night.

I had been ill with the flu and a high fever, missing five days of teaching at the elementary school. But one evening the fever finally dropped. I felt better and went right to sleep in the double bed with my husband. Our sons were in the bedroom across the hall from ours.

All at once I woke from a sound sleep. Somehow I knew a supernatural presence had entered our home. I sat up in bed as my husband slept beside me. The bedroom door was open, but I saw nothing. Yet I was totally convinced that the presence was standing in that doorway. Then a male voice spoke to me.

"I came because you knocked," he said. "And you have been chosen."

I was too stunned to reply. Even today, I don't know whether He spoke audibly or not, but I remember the things He said.

The tone of His message was kind but stern. Instead of being angry with me, He seemed very disappointed—like a loving father standing at the door of his child's room after the child broke a family rule. Though I still saw nothing, I recall thinking that He must be tall because His words were coming from near the top of the doorway.

"But I chose you," he continued. "You did not choose me."

Still I said nothing.

"And you don't need to shout. I can hear you."

I knew what He was talking about because that is what I had been doing—shouting. Since heaven was a long way off, I wanted to make sure my prayers were heard, so I had been pushing with my mind during prayer. But after I was told that *He* could hear me, I never did that again.

I don't know whether I was shouting at the time or not, but I had been asking the Lord a question. *What is my purpose in life?* On that special night, that prayer was answered.

"Your purpose in life is to be a Christian wife and mother, and you must throw away those things you have," He said.

I knew *exactly* what He meant. He wanted me to throw away the books and that horrible crystal on a chain.

Here I was face-to-face with the Lord. I guess I could have asked Him anything I wanted to ask. Yet only one question was on my mind at that moment. He'd asked that I throw away my New Age stuff, and I wanted to know when I was expected to do it.

I said, "You mean now?"

"Yes. Right now."

So I got out of bed, walked right through Jesus standing in the doorway, and went into the living room, where I kept the crystal, the chain, and the books. I gathered them up and threw them in the kitchen garbage can.

At that moment, the reality of what had just occurred hit me in the heart. I'd been calm and somewhat relaxed during my encounter with Jesus. Suddenly, I was scared to death. I'd never heard of anyone who had an experience like mine. I didn't know what to think or how to react, and I didn't know to "fear not." In fact, I didn't know a single positive Scripture verse that might have given me comfort.

Satan was doing his worst, and I was his current victim. I kept having negative thoughts like, *Things like this don't happen to ordinary people. Maybe I'm crazy.*

I was taught at my mainline church that it was wrong to go behind the altar unless you were there for a good reason, such as changing the altar flowers, cleaning the cloths behind the altar, dusting, or helping prepare communion before a service. To the lukewarm Christian I was at thirty-three, walking right through Jesus was not on my list of acceptable activities. I didn't know then that Jesus was the door to eternal life.

In my opinion I hadn't shown the Lord proper respect when I walked through that bedroom door with Jesus standing in the doorway. But at the time, all I could think about was doing what I believed the Lord wanted me to do, which was to throw away that New Age junk.

But then the Lord began teaching me truths right away—to love Him, to repent, to read the Bible, and to follow Him. He also seemed to be telling me to grow up spiritually very fast, and that meant studying the Bible seriously.

The Bible says, "Fear not," but I was frightened on the night I met Jesus. At first the unusual events scared me, and I believe my depression was brought on by fear—fear of the unknown.

But I realized that Jesus was not scary at all, once I got to know Him through God's Word, the Bible. In fact, besides being my Savior, Lord, and King, He is my best friend. I trust Him completely.

I didn't know the meaning of the important words mentioned in Deuteronomy 18. In fact, I had no interest in learning the meaning of those words and terms until after the Lord revealed himself to me. Then I discovered that the terms had to do with the occult and the Lord's commands against those practices. I began studying the meaning of terms like *abominations, enchanter, user of charms, consulter with familiar spirits, wizard,* and *necromancer.*

Maybe these important Bible verses were taught from the pulpit at our Episcopal church when I was a child and I just wasn't listening. In any case, the Lord warned against these practices, and since He didn't like them, I decided to have nothing to do with them. From that day forward, I recommended that others have nothing to do with them, either.

I had what some might call a road-to-Damascus salvation experience on the day the Lord revealed himself to me for the first time, snatching me from the jaws of Leviathan. Since then, I have loved God with all my heart, and like other former New Agers who have found the Lord, I have a strong dislike for occult and New Age literature and practices.

For a while I didn't know who spoke to me that night when I was thirty-three. I thought it was the Lord, hoped it was, but I simply wasn't sure. However, I know the identity of my visitor that night now partly because of the words He used when speaking to me.

He began by saying that He came because I knocked (Matthew 7:7 and Luke 11:9).

Then He said I was chosen (1 Peter 2: 9).

Later He said that I did not choose him; He chose me (John 15:16, 19).

I am no longer a puppet in the belly of the beast. I am a part of a chosen generation ordained to go and bring forth fruit.

I've learned a great deal since that day when Jesus stood in the doorway of our bedroom, including the fact that heaven is real. But hell is a real place, too.

Where will you spend eternity?

If you call out to God in prayer in the name of Jesus, repent of your sins, and follow Him, you will spend eternity in heaven. Choose heaven, and live in joy and peace forever.

Circle of God's Arms

MARY L. BALL

W hen can I go home?"

Mentally, I counted the times my mother had asked this question. I had been in her room only a few minutes. If my visit went as usual, she'd ask a dozen or more times before I left.

I hung her gown, turned, and plastered on my best fake smile. "Mom, I don't know. We have to speak with the doctor."

Mom huffed and turned her head. "What does he know?"

"I'm as discouraged as you. All we can do is to take one day at a time."

"One day at a time, sweet Jesus. . . ." Her singing floated throughout the room. Mother motioned for me to join her, so I chimed in with the rest of the stanzas. Our voices blended as she stopped on the words she'd forgotten and sang with all her heart the ones she remembered.

After several rounds of the song, she looked at my oldest grandson, who had accompanied me. "Who are you?" I held a breath, thankful he was old enough to understand.

"I'm your great-grandson."

I added, "He's all grown up. We used to do a lot of things together." She shook her head. The look in her eyes told me she didn't remember.

My grandson glanced at his watch, and I nodded.

"Grandma, we need to go." He was so tall that he bent awkwardly as he gave her a hug.

"Come closer." Mother pulled him toward her for a kiss. "I love you. You're not that little boy anymore that we took fishing."

"No, I guess not." He hugged her again and looked at me. We made eye contact, happy that for a few seconds she recalled.

"Good-bye, Mom. I'll be back tomorrow." My arms cradled her thin body.

"Today was a good day," my grandson said as he held the exit door for me. "Wasn't it?"

"It was all right. And at the end of our visit she remembered." I shake my head at my remark. "The reason she can recall who I am is because she sees me almost every day. You and your mom have busy lives and can't visit a lot. That's why she has trouble."

"I know, Nana. I've read a lot about Alzheimer's."

Azalea bushes lined the walkway with their pretty red blossoms welcoming everyone to the nursing home. When I was inside Mother's room, she greeted me with a bright childlike expression.

"Good morning." I bent and hugged her.

"Where have you been?" Mother looked at the rolling cart I pulled. "What's that?"

"It's your clothes." I pulled the laundry close to her wardrobe.

"When can I go home?" Mother frowns.

"I don't know, Mom. We have to talk with the doctor."

"Doctor's butt!" She puckered her mouth.

"Mom!" I pretended to be shocked but showed my amusement at the comment she had made several times during the past few months. "I hope he has a butt, or he would be odd looking."

"Well, I guess you're right. He'd be funny for sure. I just want to go home."

"Yes . . . I know."

"I would rather be home, but they treat me good." Mother sighed.

"The staff is nice to everyone." I glanced out her window at the covered deck and remembered how she used to enjoy sitting on her front porch. Silently, I fussed at myself for traveling down memory lane. Mom's voice broke through my fog of emotions.

"Where am I going to live when I leave here?" She picked away a piece of lint that only she could see from the leg of her khakis.

"Mom, you have a house." I walked over, reaching for her weathered hand. Her skin was cool under my touch. I looked into her face. My throat stung as I held back a tear that threatened to fall. My mind churns a question to God. *Why Alzheimer's, Lord?* It's the same conversation that I had with God every time I visited Mom.

Mother began her rendition of "What a Day That Will Be." I pictured her standing behind the podium at church and directed my attention to her singing.

"When my Jesus I shall see . . ." She repeated parts of the chorus three times, then stopped. "When can I go home?"

"I wish I had an answer, Mom." Once again, I smiled. I wanted her to believe everything was fine.

Slowly, I strolled outside. My lungs filled and deflated a heavy breath of relief that I was able to leave without her crying. "Thank you, Lord. It hurts to see her upset."

I tossed the rolling cart into the trunk of my car and scooted inside. Mindlessly, I put the key in the ignition.

My shoulders slumped. Tears eased down my cheek. When my sorrow finished filling the car, I glanced around. An oak tree offered shade while a bird perched on a limb sang a chirpy song. I smiled, appreciating the feathery beauties God created for His children.

"Mom liked to watch the birds." Too quickly, my concentration was back on Mother and her illness. I pressed my lips tight. "Almost two years." Twenty months since the last time she dressed herself. Only to hear her talk, she would tell you just this morning she picked out her outfit. I'd learned long ago that things are different in her mind.

"Lord, I've prayed. I've cried out to you. I've given this over to you. Why am I still burdened with grief? Why can't I find the peace that you offer?"

My spirit quickened. As if Jesus were beside me in the passenger's seat, my mind became immersed with His Spirit. "You haven't completely turned it over to me. You keep taking it back. Your tears and fretting prevent me from helping."

I straightened up as the wisdom of God's words covered me. "Lord, this is what you meant when you instructed the disciples to write about casting cares."

The revelation He offered was a beacon. Jesus opened my eyes to something I had easily overlooked. Giving my burdens to the Lord meant that I had to turn them loose in every way.

I had to let go of the anxiety. I rubbed my forehead. Had I let the mental stress I faced control my life?

"Instead of giving my woes to you, Lord, I was cradling my sadness."

Now I realized the deeper meaning of the verses.

I started the car and backed out as 1 Peter 5:7 played in my conscience: "Give all your worries and cares to God, for he cares about you."

When I turned onto the highway, I was in awe of how God had rekindled my spirit and heightened my awareness. I thought I was a strong spiritual person, but God reminded me that His word is always enlightening.

On the way home I prayed. I asked the Lord to give me the strength to release this burden that I was tired of carrying. I petitioned God to make me aware of any instances where I may be near a point of pulling my problem away from the circle of His arms. As I sealed the prayer in Jesus' name, I relaxed in the fact that I had a new grasp on the complexity of casting my cares. On my next visit I prayed for the strength to leave my worries behind.

As time goes on, Mother has good and bad days, and I have moments when I almost give in to sadness. But thank God, I haven't.

On Mother's good days, I leave the facility with praise in my heart. During her bad times, I thank the Lord, for He helps me to have grace.

Nothing is too big or too small for God. I applaud the stories of healing and deliverance, but there are also circumstances where God shows His love that simply cannot be discounted.

At this time in my life it was a small miracle. I'm so grateful that one afternoon the Lord brought my attention to the fact that when I gave in to my sorrows and focused on the hurt, I was preventing His peace from wrapping around me.

This situation that my family faces isn't a new one, nor is it easy. The Lord has used my heartache to show me where I was missing the mark. I can't be assured that my life will always be smooth, but I know that I now understand the proper way to hand my cares over. I rest assured in the belief that all the worries coming my way will be in the circle of God's arms.

Face-to-Face with Jesus

SHARILYNN HUNT

When my husband's company transferred him to a different state, our emotions were challenged. Friends, previous co-workers, even casual acquaintances vanished from our daily lives. Our families lived across the country, and I had trouble coping with the adjustment of the move.

My husband, David, worked long hours, and I was now alone with our newborn son and strong-willed three-year-old daughter after having been a working mom. My loneliness turned to resentment toward David and his schedule while we all settled into a new routine. Our marriage became strained as we attempted to adjust to the move, his job, and a new baby.

I began to vent my anger toward my daughter. Too many harsh words and spankings revealed a mother unable to cope. I needed a counselor. One day, I fell sobbing to my knees and cried out to God. "I need help to deal with all of this—please, help me!"

Help came in an unexpected form.

A few days later, a neighbor asked, "Would you like to go to a Bible study near here? It's in someone's home, and we've just been meeting for a few weeks."

I desperately wanted to get to know other young mothers in the area, but a Bible study? I knew little about the Bible, but since I had a college degree, I felt it would be a good educational experience. A local church provided childcare, and I agreed to try it.

I began to study basic Christianity with other stay-at-home moms. Most of us lived in or near our new subdivision, had moved from different parts of the country, and had various backgrounds. The group consisted of fifteen women from all denominations of faith.

We had no idea God handpicked us for this time in life, and with His stamp of grace, He would move most of us to other cities in the future. I felt quite anxious in this type of setting, but I received a warm welcome from the others, which reassured me.

Along with weekly meetings, we had homework assignments, which we would discuss in our sessions. Every week I grilled the leader with questions, which she patiently answered.

The prayer time at the end of our morning together astonished me. These women comfortably prayed aloud for others in need and believed God listened to them. Week after week I heard praise reports of answered prayers.

I listened to them pray around a circle, but when my turn came I could not speak. Fear gripped me. My heart pounded and I sat with clammy hands until my turn passed. I had never prayed aloud with anyone before. When I was growing up, my father would say grace when we had company, but that was it for prayer together. How could I talk to God in front of all these people? They seemed to believe Jesus heard them, too.

At my turn, I would say, "Pass," and felt assured God would never expect me, an unqualified person, to pray in front of others.

For three months I asked questions about the living Christ, and then one day invited the leader to have lunch with me. I prayed a prayer of salvation with her, but I had little understanding of the spiritual impact of the day. After all, what could a little prayer do? I had doubted if Jesus still existed. But at the end of our visit, I closed the door with an unusual feeling of peace in my heart.

That evening, the kids slept while my husband and I watched television—a normal routine. My weekly lesson was in my lap, along with my open Bible. Nothing odd or unusual occurred until I saw *Him*.

Time stopped. In one moment, the object of my earlier prayer came in a vision. Jesus and I were face to face.

No one else existed in the room while I looked into the purest eyes of love, which penetrated my soul. I cannot say to this day the color of Jesus' eyes as they sparkled. The vision showed His face with shoulder-length hair and dark eyebrows. I could see a white garment on His shoulders.

Jesus smiled. His presence carried strength, authority, and power. I felt unconditional love flow from Him, and I realized that He knew all about my doubts, feelings, and search for a deeper spiritual life. I experienced a supernatural encounter with the divine, one who needed no words to convey His living presence.

I sat spellbound until the vision disappeared. Without a word to David, I ran upstairs to the bedroom, thinking the Son of God wanted to spend more time with me.

The room was dark and quiet except for the excited beating of my heart as I sat on the bed.

What just happened? Why would Jesus appear to me? He knew I questioned His existence, yet I wanted to believe. He never appeared again.

How can a person return to a normal routine after such an encounter?

For days I could not tell anyone about this experience, not even my husband. It seemed too holy—too intimate and personal. I had been touched by God's love, and it had left an imprint on my heart. I experienced a love for Jesus unlike anything before—as if I had become a new bride on a honeymoon.

I could not wait to attend the Bible study the next week. Now I received the true message of the Scriptures we studied, and I felt a different connection with the other women. I spent hours doing my lessons and reading God's Word, which came to life. I loved my family even more and wanted to do extra things for them.

I had a smoking habit at the time, and I continued to smoke. But I found it odd that I could no longer stand the taste. The desire for cigarettes had left, and I threw them out. The habit of using foul language ceased as the words felt unclean when I released them.

My emotions underwent a complete change, as well. Peace and joy entered our home. After a few months, I realized I *had* become a new creation in Christ at the age of twenty-seven.

I began to share my personal experience with others. Fear no longer gripped me when we prayed together in the study group. I began to pray short prayers and believed God heard them.

I remember the moment when I took my last alcoholic drink at my husband's office party. I was telling one of his co-workers about Jesus, and I looked at the glass in my hand with different eyes. I set it down and realized many pleasures from my former life no longer satisfied me. The presence of the Holy One had impacted my core of existence.

Our Sunday routine changed when I decided to take the children to the same church that had provided childcare during the week. The church began a bus route to our neighborhood, and I signed up. We rode the bus for a few weeks until my husband decided to join us for the services as he began his own spiritual search.

I loved the fellowship of other believers. The congregation extended their friendship to become adopted grandparents, aunts, and uncles for our small children. Communion became a personal, holy sacrament to me. Learning the hymns of my Savior, Redeemer, and Lord brought worship into my life. The songs on Easter Sunday thrilled me as I understood the truth of the Resurrection. I wanted to shout to everyone, "He's alive today!" Christmas became a birthday celebration instead of just an exchange of presents or focused on Santa Claus.

Within a few months, my husband also accepted Christ. We joined the neighborhood church and began to rebuild our marriage on godly principles. God had taken my prayer of despair and turned it into a life of joy.

The Bible study ended after two years, and we called the area on the map "God's Little Acre." Over the time, many of the husbands and children had also been affected from our time together. Two couples went into full-time ministry.

My quest to learn God's Word continued in various studies and seminary classes. We moved to two other states while I ministered in many venues and reentered a career as a medical social worker. I taught neighborhood Bible studies, spoke to various women's groups, led workshops, prayed for governmental leaders, and spoke about prayer before five thousand women at a conference in Russia.

God changed my fears of prayer into a passion for prayer. Jesus' face-to-face encounter truly had transformed me from the inside out and changed my life.

God Can Save Anyone

MARTY PRUDHOMME

If God can save my brother, Bush, He can save anyone.

We grew up in a typical 1950s middle-class home. Our parents took us to church and taught us to believe in God, although we didn't develop a personal relationship with Jesus. I had a hunger to know more about God, but He always seemed so far away.

Bush, on the other hand, was not interested in things pertaining to God. As far back as I can remember, he was rebellious.

In school Bush scored above genius on IQ tests. He could remember everything he read and began to think he knew more than our parents. Our dad, a printer for a department store in town, had a third-grade education. Our mom went to business school and became a secretary. Bush looked down on our parents and didn't want to hear anything they had to say. His attitude caused constant tension in our home, and the seeds of rebellion grew in him like wildfire.

When Bush was seventeen, tragedy struck. Driving home one night around midnight, he hit and killed an elderly man who was walking on a dark stretch of road. The judge ruled it an accident and released Bush, but I couldn't imagine how painful that must have been for him. I believe he hardened his heart as a self-defense mechanism.

After that ordeal, Bush couldn't wait to leave home. As soon as he graduated from high school, he found a job about eighty miles away, driving a dump truck for a construction company. Then one afternoon in the middle of a terrible rainstorm, he hit two little girls as they ran across a busy highway. One was badly injured; the other was brain damaged.

Bush lost his job, but no criminal charges were brought against him. The construction company's insurance paid for the damages; however, I don't think Bush ever knew the long-term repercussions to the girls. He never spoke about what happened.

By the mid 1960s, America was embroiled in the Vietnam War. Hoping to dodge the draft, Bush went to college. After several years of separation, he and I ended up together at the University of Southwestern Louisiana. I enjoyed spending time with my big brother, and when we weren't in class, we were inseparable.

Unfortunately, our time together didn't last. Because Louisiana schools still had lots of rules and regulations—which Bush couldn't deal with—he dropped out of college. He may have been very intelligent, but he lacked common sense and had little wisdom. Before long he received his A1 classification, which meant he would soon be drafted into the army. Not thrilled with the idea of the army, Bush joined the marine reserves.

He attended boot camp in California and then came back to Louisiana, where he went to weekend drills once a month. Bush soon tired of the monotony of drills and quit the reserves. He didn't use much common sense in that decision. The army drafted him and off he went to Vietnam, where he was wounded twice in the same leg.

The drugs and abuses of war left Bush bitter and more determined than ever to reject any type of authority. He bought a Harley Davidson motorcycle and took to the road, working as a mechanic. He would stay in one place long enough to make a little money, then have a disagreement with the boss and take off again to some new place. Bush loved the freedom of the open road. I heard from him only when he called me from a friend's telephone.

In his early forties, Bush finally decided to settle down and get married. He and Cindy, a girl from northern California, had a little boy they named Justin. Bush confided in me, "I finally have someone to love who is completely mine—he is wonderful."

I was happy for Bush; he seemed content. When our dad died, Bush and Cindy came to visit. It was difficult to lose my dad but so good to see them.

Before Dad's death, my husband, Bill, and I had accepted Jesus as Lord and Savior. We were headed for a divorce when Jesus came into our lives. He healed our hearts from past hurts and saved our marriage.

When I tried to share this good news with Bush, he cut me off. "I had my own experience with God. I saw God in a cloud with bright lights. It was a great feeling."

He went on to describe what sounded like a drug-induced hallucination. He made it clear he didn't want to hear anything else about God.

When it became evident that Mom could no longer take care of her house, Bush and Cindy moved in to help her out. However, tensions flared, so Bill and I decided to add a room onto our home for Mom. She told Bush, "If you will wait until Bill finishes the addition, you can have my house."

Cindy hated Louisiana. She had never experienced such oppressive heat or mosquitoes and wanted to go home to California. Then one day Bush blew up, cursed at Mom, and decided they were leaving, even though they didn't have a place to live in California.

"We won't have room for Mom until the addition is finished," I told Bush. "Just be patient. You can get her house, sell it, and have a nest egg to start over in California."

He wouldn't listen. "No, it's taking too long. I can't stand living with that old lady. We're leaving."

Once again, Bush had no patience or wisdom. I made sure he had our phone number. "Promise you'll call when you get settled. I want to know how you all are doing. Remember, I love you very much."

A year went by without a word from Bush. I tracked down a phone number for Cindy's mother, and she told me Cindy had taken the baby, divorced Bush, and remarried. Cindy did not want to see Bush, nor did she know where he was.

I continued to search for him and even went through the Social Security Administration, to no avail. Twenty years passed. All the while, I prayed that God would keep him alive and save his soul.

Then one day my nephew called. "Aunt Marty, we found Uncle Bush. He's still in California. I'm going to see him."

I was ecstatic. "Find out all the details. Tell him I love him and have never stopped searching for him."

We learned that Bush had been heartbroken over the divorce and lost several years to drugs. More recently, he had been in an accident. While he was sitting on his motorcycle at a red light, a huge dump truck ran the light and plowed over him, pinning him under the truck. His leg and hip were crushed; he had several other broken bones and severe head injuries. He lay in a coma for eight weeks. After months of rehabilitation, he was left in a wheelchair.

The court settlement included a lump sum of money and a monthly income for the rest of his life to pay for medical care. For the first time, Bush bought a home and had a phone—which was how we found him through a computer search.

When I went to visit Bush, all I could do was love on him. Bush kept asking, "Why are you so good to me?"

I told him, "I love you, Bush, and have never stopped searching for you. No matter how long it has been or what has happened to you, I still love you."

I tried to talk to him about the Lord.

Bush turned red and cursed as he yelled, "I don't want to hear about any of that God stuff."

His venom shocked me. "Bush, I don't deserve to be talked to that way, and I don't want you to ever curse at me again."

As I left to go home I asked him, "If you are wrong about God, wouldn't you want to know?"

Bush thought a minute. "Yeah, I'd want to know."

I thought, *Okay, Lord, you heard that.*

Every year I visited Bush, and then he became ill with a septic infection and nearly died. Ricky, Bush's friend, had been living with Bush rent-free plus salary. He was supposed to take care of Bush and the house, but his neglect almost cost Bush his life.

I flew out to see him in the hospital, praying all the way, "God give me wisdom; tell me what to say to him."

The first week Bush was hallucinating. Two weeks later he was moved to a rehab facility. During the day I searched for responsible healthcare aides, and each evening I spent with Bush. I would have an attendant get him into the car, and we would drive to a nearby park and talk.

The Lord prompted me to ask Bush, "Do you realize how close to death you came?"

"It was a close call. That Ricky went off and left me to die. If other friends had not checked on me, I would be dead."

"Bush, I believe God was looking out for you because He has plans for your future. The doctor said if your friends had not brought you in when they did, you would have died the next day."

Bush was finally listening.

"I want to tell you a story about three men on crosses at Calvary. Two of the men were thieves. They didn't go to church, and they probably didn't know anything about the Bible. One man cursed God and died, but the other cried out for mercy. Jesus looked at him with great compassion and said, 'Today you will be with me in paradise.'"

As I spoke, the Lord's presence enveloped us. There was such sweetness; Bush felt it, too.

"That second man is you, Bush; you have no religion or faith, but if you will ask the Lord to come into your life, He will fill up all the empty places and heal your wounded heart. He will fill you with His love. Jesus has always loved you, Bush, and has waited for you to turn to Him."

Tears filled his eyes as I told him of God's goodness.

Bush had a problem with how God decides who goes to heaven. I used Ricky as an example. "Would you allow Ricky back into your house? Don't you have the right to decide who comes in and who does not? You only allow people who are your friends into your home. So why would God let someone into heaven who is not His friend?"

His expression told me he understood. In that moment, I was able to lead my bitter, angry, lost, hurting brother in the sinner's prayer. He repented of all his sins and asked Jesus to come in and be Lord of his life. As he wept, I said, "God has forgiven all of your sins. Do you think you could forgive Ricky? God doesn't want you to be bound by bitterness ever again."

Bush forgave Ricky.

Now when I visit Bush I read Scripture to him, and he gets teary-eyed as he hears God's Word. He still needs constant nursing care and is still wheelchair bound, but he is no longer bitter or angry. God has washed away all the years of hurt and pain. Bush is at peace. He jokes, he laughs, and he likes to have people and children around him. My brother's life has been transformed by the love of Jesus.

What a marvelous God! If He can save Bush, He can save absolutely anyone.

God Had Other Plans

EMMA CHAMBERS

I'm going to spend years in a mental hospital."

I had run into a closet in my bedroom as an eight-year-old, trying to get away from my father. As he stood outside the closet ranting, his words cut like knives, shredding any feeling that I was loveable or worthy to be alive on this earth.

One thought came to me in that closet: *Because of this moment and all the pain inside, in the future I'm going to spend years in a mental hospital.*

After that day, my battle with bitterness, unforgiveness, self-loathing, and depression intensified. I was able to excel in school, go to church, and even laugh often. But beneath the laughter a shattered heart announced, *You are unlovable!*

My father reminded me of that with his harsh words, perfectionistic expectations, and hours-long tirades telling me how awful I was as a human being.

Thoughts of death filled my mind, but I was too afraid to act on them. God seemed far away, and I felt unloved by Him, since He refused to rescue me from my hellish existence.

My mother showed some love, but I couldn't understand why she wouldn't speak up or scream at my father to stop abusing their children. I remember her face outside that closet, passively looking on as my father berated me. I wondered why she didn't say or do anything. One day when I asked the Lord that question yet again, He said, "She did; she prayed."

Perhaps those prayers saved my life.

I married someone like my father, who assaulted me with cutting words because of his own wounds. Two years into our marriage, he said he didn't love me and never had. He decided he still loved his old girlfriend.

During that time, I received Jesus as my Savior. I went to counseling sessions, deliverance services, and prayer meetings to deal with the pain that still resided in my soul. My husband's old girlfriend decided not to leave her husband, so my man decided he did love me, and that we should try to stay together.

Still, the unkind words continued, and I volleyed mean words right back.

While I was pregnant with my first child, my twenty-one-year-old sister committed suicide. She had battled paranoid schizophrenia, which my perfectionistic father couldn't tolerate. He ranted at her, attempting to eradicate her mental illness. She was in and out of the hospital and often had issues with the police when her mental breakdowns occurred in public places.

I blamed my father for my sister's death. I felt he had pushed her to it, and I wanted him to admit this.

"If she hadn't done it, I would have had to kill myself," he said.

80

That day I realized how truly sick my father was.

After that, God dealt with me about forgiving my father. I apologized to him for holding on to bitterness. I told him I forgave him for everything he'd done when I was a child.

He couldn't say, "I'm sorry." He could only reply, "I did the best I could." This was true considering the fact that he'd had an abusive, alcoholic father and a mother with severe OCD and depression.

For so long I thought my misery resulted from how my father had treated me, but God revealed that it was because of my own bitterness. As forgiveness took over, my relationship with my father began to heal.

This also helped in my relationship with my husband. He still said words that stung, but I learned to ask God, "What do *you* have to say?" His sweet, comforting words brought hope and healing. And I no longer felt I had to return unkind words.

I continued to battle depression and at times suicidal thoughts, especially during a horrendous bout with postpartum depression when I felt that because of my husband's continued verbal abuse in front of our baby, the best course would be to take both of our lives—our baby's and mine. God rescued me from that dangerous thinking.

I tried antidepressants, but they offered minimal relief. One day a doctor who was prescribing medication asked me, "When do you think your depression started?"

Although I thought my depression was based in my father's cruel treatment, these words came out of my mouth: "I was born depressed."

A while later I went to a seminar where the speaker asked if we were wanted when we were born. I realized my mother had been depressed when she was carrying me, which contributed to this sense of having been born depressed. As people prayed over me, I pictured Jesus in my mother's womb holding me and saying, "Emma, even if no one else wants you to be born, I want you to be born."

Those words cut through so much pain inside of me.

A second turning point came after I had cried out to God that I didn't feel loved by Him. "The Bible may say you 'so loved the world,' but I need to have you tell me that by my name."

Not long after that I was in a prayer meeting where people were learning to recognize God's voice. I gave a prayer request unrelated to feeling unloved. Suddenly one of the women said this several times as a word from the Lord: "Emma, know that I love you."

God gave me what I had asked for—a statement of love that included my name.

A third victory came after I had forgotten to do a favor for a friend. It was a minor issue, but since I was raised in a perfectionistic home, I felt my friend would reject me forever.

Shame wrapped around me, even as I went to another Bible study. There we were instructed to find a partner and wash each other's feet. The lady who washed my feet spoke powerful words—words that were spoken from the Lord through her: "Emma, I will never be ashamed to call you my daughter."

At that moment I remembered a childhood incident when I had failed to wrap the lettuce perfectly in the refrigerator. My father came into the bathroom and threw the head of lettuce at me.

In the midst of his rage, he said, "If someone came up to me on the street and asked, 'Is she your daughter?' I would be too ashamed to say yes."

I realized the recent incident had triggered this sense that one day, like my father, God would reject me for all my imperfections. Those words, "I will never be ashamed to call you my daughter," did wonders in the healing process.

Then when my daughter was twenty-one years old—the same age my sister died—she battled suicidal thoughts after being raped. My heart broke further as she rejected the Lord. I felt shame that I had passed along suicidal tendencies and even a depressive personality.

In the midst of my daughter's battle, a good friend's husband—a pastor—committed suicide.

I felt bereft. How could my daughter, who had rejected God, be protected from suicide when this man of God who gave hope and encouragement to so many was not?

I pleaded with God to spare my daughter's life. The only promise I received was that He would be with me—no matter what. (He did deliver her.)

During my wrestling, I wondered if suicide would suddenly swoop down on me, like it did on this man. I went to my husband with my fears. He gave me 1 Corinthians 10:13: "When you are tempted, [God] will show you a way out so that you can endure."

"That pastor was given the way of escape, but he refused to take it," my husband said.

I went back to seeking the Lord. He spoke these words to me: "You now have mental health. I want you to work with others to help them."

Soon after, I looked for jobs on psychiatric wards. God was leading me away from working as a nurse, which centered on medications, so when I saw a job opening for a mental health tech, I went through the application and hiring process, and soon found myself on a psychiatric ward helping people deal with hopelessness.

I've worked as a mental health tech on the psychiatric ward at my local hospital for the past thirteen and a half years.

Often I think of those words that went through my mind in that closet years ago: "I'm going to spend years in a mental hospital."

Those words came true, but not in the way I imagined. I believe it was Satan's plan that I be there as a patient—depressed, defeated, discouraged.

But God had other plans.

Some days I wonder how I'm able to deal with the intensity of what I've observed on our acute-care psychiatric unit. God has given me strength, words to say, and unconditional love for the patients. I've seen so many lives transformed from hopelessness to embracing hope. He's given me courage to share my story and to tell them, "You, too, can be healed." He's led me to learn to play the guitar and allowed me to reach the patients not only with spoken words but with words I sing.

I thank God our hospital believes in helping the patients with their spiritual as well as their physical and emotional lives. As I allow God to speak words of hope to my patients through me, I hear what I'm saying, and those words keep hope alive in my own soul. This was especially true in 2012 after my youngest brother committed suicide while dealing with chronic pain.

My miracle didn't happen overnight, but it has still been a miracle. Years ago all I could think about was how crushed I felt by the cruelty of others. Now I want to help people with their brokenness. A favorite verse I pass along to my patients is this: "He heals the brokenhearted and bandages their wounds" (Psalm 147:3). My life testifies to that truth.

What came to mind so many years ago in that closet turned into a calling from God for me to comfort and help others be healed with the comfort and healing touch that I have received from Him (2 Corinthians 1:4). What a privilege it is to receive a miracle and then help others believe that God longs to give one to them, as well.

Walking on the Water

NANETTE FRIEND

Taking my usual afternoon walk on the prison "walk-jog" path that day, attempting to escape the relentless cursing, hostility, and often depressive attitudes of the other inmates, I desperately cried out, *I don't understand, God! What do you want from me? Either take me from this world, or do something with me!*

Depressed to the point of suicidal thoughts, I reached out with the intensity of a seriously distraught yet determined woman. *You will have to change me, Lord, because I don't know how!*

Shuffling along, I picked up the pace so others wouldn't see the tears running down my face.

I was a businesswoman, mother of four, and grandmother to four young boys, but I'd left that behind when I walked through the massive gates of the Women's State Correctional facility five months earlier. Though at first I was filled with constant fear and anxiety, I had now somewhat adjusted to the everyday life I was destined to endure for the rest of my sentence. However, now I was more terrified than ever of what was to come next. How would I ever survive in the outside world after this?

I was a thief, a cheat, and a liar. Who would ever hire me or believe me again? Who would ever trust or have confidence in me? Who would ever forgive me for the sins I had committed? I had lied to, stolen from, and manipulated so many innocent people. I knew my life would never be the same again.

Don't you understand, God? I won't even be able to work at a gas station because I won't be trusted to handle other people's money.

As I continued walking briskly on the hot black asphalt, I gradually became aware of the appearance of "black ice," or a mirage, before me. Believing the bright sun was reflecting on the pavement, I continued to gaze at the movement of the reflection well ahead of me. However, I soon noticed a "rippling" effect of the illusion, giving me the sense that small waves of water were now surrounding me. I slowed my pace and then stopped. It appeared that with each step I took, the water separated around the outline of my foot.

Was I imagining this? I looked around to see if other walkers also noticed the "water" on the path.

Do you trust me?

Okay, now I was beginning to think I was losing my mind. I recalled only one other time that a voice, a thought, deep within my mind was speaking to me. That was at a time in my life when I had actually attempted suicide.

Do you trust me? The thought penetrated even deeper.

"I don't know, God. I want to, but I'm afraid."

Not wanting to give the impression to the yard security or others that I was unaware of the physical world around me, I cautiously continued to walk forward, taking one slow step after another.

Will you walk on the water with me?

I stopped again. But with each cautious step into "the water," I was well aware of the solid ground beneath me.

I was reminded of the story of Peter walking on the water during the terrific storm in Matthew 14:24–32.

I knew what God was asking of me. He wanted me to turn my focus strictly to Him, to accept Him as my saving grace, to trust Him with all of my soul, and to ask Him even deeper into my heart.

Only a few months before, I had fallen to my knees on the floor of my prison cell and had accepted Jesus into my heart. I had wanted Him to comfort me, love me, forgive me, and accept me, despite the sinner that I was. I wanted to know who He was and for Him to teach me all that He could. I was desperate and hopeless, filled with great remorse and regret for all of the horrible things I had done. I was truly seeking all these things of Him.

But now He was seeking something of me.

"I don't know, God. I want to trust you, but I'm afraid you'll let me down." I remembered physical, sexual, and mental abuse I had endured since the time I was a small girl. I had trusted my father, my two ex-husbands, as well as many other men in my life—but they had all betrayed me. I had been beaten, lied to, cheated on, and stolen from. The people I thought loved me the most shot at, spit on, stalked, and seduced me. How could I ever trust anyone again?

"Okay, God, but please don't let me down. I can't take any more. If I do this thing that you ask of me, please hold on to my hand. I'm not strong enough yet. Don't let go of me, Jesus. If you let go of me, I will never believe or trust anyone again. Hold on really tight."

I felt like a little girl again, holding on to the hand of my grandfather when he used to walk beside me. Papa was six feet tall and had very long legs. I was only two to three years old, but I remember running alongside him, trying to keep up with his stride. Until the very day he passed from this world, I had always cherished Papa with the innocence and faith that only a child can have.

I gained more confidence with each step now. I imagined that I was truly walking on the Sea of Galilee, walking into the arms of Jesus. I knew I had to keep my eyes on Him, straight ahead of me, or I would begin to sink.

The godly vision caused me to feel instantly relieved, and yet so very cautious at the same time. I wanted to tread lightly, but gain confidence and reassurance that Jesus would be there for me.

"Okay, God, I'm ready now. I don't know how to do this, but I will trust you. What do you want me to do? Where do I go from here?"

His words came softly. . . .

Someday you will guide teenagers and speak before thousands.

Now I knew I must have certainly misunderstood that message. I was a single mom, and my four children had recently left their teen years. I had no desire whatsoever to work with teenagers again. I also felt I should never speak or teach others about anything at all. "Lord, I am a liar and a thief. I am the lowest of all. Who would ever believe me? What would I ever have to say to them?"

The message continued, *They will know because you know.*

I suddenly remembered watching a television broadcast of Joyce Meyer, a Christian evangelist. Before my conviction, and in my relentless search for hope and comfort, I had occasionally tuned in to watch this woman of God. Not really sure that I even liked her, let alone understood her, I was finally fed up one day. I didn't know who the Israelites were, or this mountain she was talking about that they kept walking around . . . for forty years, no less!

What kind of God would tell His people to do that?

I shouted out to the television set, "Lady, you have no idea what I have been through in my life. You have your perfect Christian family and your perfect Christian husband, your perfect hair and your perfect clothes. Until you have walked in my shoes, *don't* tell me about your God because He doesn't exist for me!"

As I jumped up to turn the channel on my old console television, Joyce began talking about her abusive father, her pregnancy at an early age, and the physical abuse of her first husband. She explained that she had been forced to call her family to beg for bus fare so she could travel back across the country to come home. She went on to tell how she met her current *Christian* husband while washing her Volkswagen Beetle in her driveway one day, wearing only a bikini and drinking a beer. I knew that Ms. Meyer had four children, and I also had four children. She was telling my story. I slowly went back to my seat on the couch and began to absorb the message she was teaching.

I now knew what God meant. He wanted me to understand that people going through great fear, pain, and trouble would believe me because they would know I had walked in their shoes. He wanted me to tell them He was still real today, just as He has always been. He wanted me to tell people to believe in Him again. I got it.

"Okay, God. I understand, but I have a lot to learn. I will take this journey, but don't let go of me."

God provided me with that image sixteen years ago. I was released from prison two months later, having served seven months of my twelve-month sentence. God filled my life with many more lessons, miracles, visions, and teachings. He blessed me with jobs and opportunities I never dreamed possible.

My fears of unemployment never materialized. I have worked with a doctor's office, an insurance company, and a counseling center. I've worked with the mentally challenged and with foster children. I became manager of a Christian youth center, working with and mentoring teenagers, and loving every minute of it! I volunteered for "Rites of Passage," a last-chance program for at-risk teenage girls who had been court-ordered to either attend the program or go to jail.

I volunteered at a battered women's shelter, and I currently lead a women's Bible study each week at the local county jail. I have written many inspirational articles for newspapers and contributed to the book *Stories of Faith and Courage from Prison*. Today I am speaking and writing a series of books regarding the many miracles and visions God has given me.

God *is* real. He is the same God today that He has always been! He only wants us to come to Him . . . and trust Him. He has a plan and a promise for the very least of us, if we will only allow him to fulfill it (Jeremiah 29:11).

I know it's true because He revealed His plan for me the day He asked me to walk on water on the sidewalk of a correctional facility.

Taking Away the Desire

CAROL NASH SMITH

Quit drinking or you are in for a bad time of it. You will have heart problems, stomach problems, liver problems, and a sorry social life. You might as well face facts, Carol. You are an alcoholic, and you are ruining your life."

I think I knew this ultimatum from my doctor was coming, but I had resisted hearing it. I never drank at work or before work, because as a schoolteacher, I knew it would be the end of me professionally if I did. But I drank every night until I passed out.

I could go without alcohol, if necessary, when I had to take the high school kids on overnight trips such as journalism conventions, but just as soon as I hit the door to my home, I was drinking again. I did a pretty good job of covering up my nasty little secret with my students, but looking back I am amazed that they didn't guess, and maybe some of them did with the telephone calls to my house at night when I was "terribly happy" on the phone, or times when I just didn't make much sense. I would pass it off the next day by saying I was really tired or that my husband and I were in a really silly mood that night.

The kids were benevolent. They liked me, so they didn't want to believe anything bad about me. I didn't, either, but the truth was killing me.

The doctor wanted to send me to a rehab facility for three months.

"No way!" I told him.

I couldn't afford to take that much time off school, and besides, I didn't think the administrators would look kindly on my reasons for that sort of leave of absence. I think my doctor understood my reasoning, because he agreed to my going to AA. I wasn't too happy about that, either, but I found an AA group that met about fifteen miles out of town, where I thought no one would know me. I was determined to not attend meetings where perhaps someone would see me and the word would get out to the school. All of this is very silly, but alcoholics are ego-driven people.

I thought of myself as a good person, but obviously I was weak in many areas. I had always considered myself a Christian, yet I could not get a handle on this drinking problem. My need to drink was stronger than my will to give it up. This had gone on for many years. I was on my third divorce; it is easy to see that my personal life was a mess. My spiritual life was a mess. My finances were also a big mess. I was going down like the *Titanic*. Could it be that drinking had something to do with the messes?

The first thing that happened when I decided to try AA was that I was introduced to some people by phone in the Diamond Head group, the one about fifteen miles from town. One woman I spoke with agreed to be my sponsor. She was convinced that I was "teachable," she said. I was not sure what that meant or how she came to that conclusion, but I was pleased that she would take me on.

I was frightened at the first meeting. When I pulled into the parking lot, I saw someone I knew drive up, and I tried to back out of the meeting. But my sponsor talked me out of going home.

The person I knew decided not to attend the meeting after all, so I got off the hook on that one. I eventually learned that I couldn't let the fact that I knew people who were attending meetings stop me from going, but it was all so new to me, and I was trying very hard to be "anonymous."

The meeting went well, and I saw there was nothing to be afraid of. The people were welcoming and kind and made me feel at home. However, I was still having a hard time thinking that I was an alcoholic. My reasoning: I don't like labels. Yeah, right.

After the meeting, Jo, my new sponsor, and I went to have coffee, and she talked with me about the program and the steps. She asked me if I was ready to quit drinking. I told her that I knew I had to, but I really didn't know if I could. She explained that in the program, we believe in a Higher Power who can take this craving from us. We have to ask Him to do that.

I told her that I had prayed for Him to help me before and He hadn't. She said, "Maybe you were asking all wrong."

"What do you mean?" I asked, astonished.

"You asked for help," she said. "You didn't ask Him to take the desire from you. You have to let go and let God take the craving for drink completely away from you."

I sat there for a minute feeling overwhelmed. "Are you telling me that God will completely take the compulsion to drink away from me?"

"I am," she answered.

"I have trouble believing that," I said.

"You don't even have to believe me," she answered. "Just act like you do. Do what I tell you to do and pray as if you believe. Get down on your knees and turn your craving over to God. Tell Him to take it away from you from that moment on. See what happens."

I went home with a million things going on in my mind. I wanted this. I really did. I wanted to be able to live without drinking. I could do what she said, but what if it didn't work?

Then I realized that I absolutely couldn't think about the negative. I was just going to do it like Jo said.

And so I did.

I didn't hear God's voice. There was no thunder, no lightning. I didn't have a vision.

But I did not want a drink.

Not that night. Not the next day, nor the next night, nor the next day, nor the next night.

I have not had a drink nor have I wanted one for twenty-one years now. The only explanation I have for it is that I got down on my knees and turned my craving for alcohol over to God, asking Him to take it away from me. To me, this is a miracle. Nothing I could have done on my own could have produced this effect.

Since that time, I have not had blackouts. I have not embarrassed myself. I have led a much happier life. My finances are in good shape. My personal life is great. I have married a really good man, and we are in church every Sunday. I volunteer in the church. I work in our food pantry and visit with the people who come in to get food. Sometimes the people who come in have problems with alcohol. I can relate to them. I have a story to tell them.

Their problems don't have to be about alcohol, however, for me to tell them about the redeeming qualities of our Lord. We pray together, and we talk about God's overarching love for all of His children. When we ask Him in the right spirit, He will answer our prayer. He has made that promise to us, and I know He does what He says He will do!

Miracles don't have to come in dramatic form. Mine was dramatic to me, but no one else knew anything about it unless I began telling him or her about it. My big life change was not evident to anyone except my closest friends.

However, it has been huge to me and to my family. And I think it has been enormous to the outcome of my life. I am no longer ego-driven. My greatest pleasure now comes in helping others and doing what I can for a better world.

I am a strong proponent of Alcoholics Anonymous. The program is fantastic in its simple approach to ridding its participants of the craving of alcohol. It works. And it works by tenets that should be obvious to all of us. Turn your life over to God. Love your fellow man. Do not wrong him. Don't drink today. Go to meetings.

It no longer hurts to say, "My name is Carol. I am an alcoholic."

That is not just a label. It is a reminder that if I decide to drink an alcoholic drink today, I will again be the mess I was twenty-one years ago, and I don't ever want to go back to being that Carol. I am much happier with the sober Carol I am today. And I thank God for that.

My Weight Destination

MICHELLE J. WELCOME

I stared down at the scale. My hope faded as the number 189 popped up on the screen. I collapsed on the bed. Despair filled my heart.

"What is going on, Lord? Why is it that no matter what I do I reach a certain point, I can't seem to move further?"

A few years earlier, the Lord had spoken to me as I worked out in our family gym. "Every time you step on the treadmill, you will trample the enemy under your feet! Thirteen, fourteen, and one hundred and fifty."

When the words were spoken to my spirit, I knew instantly what the Lord meant. My exercising was warfare. It would allow me to put the enemy where he belonged: under my feet (Genesis 3:15).

But the part that really stuck with me was *thirteen, fourteen.* At the time, I was a size 22 on a bad day and between 18 and

20 on an average day. Between the bloating and inflammation, I could never predict what size I would be able to wear on a given day. Therefore, getting down to a size 13/14 would have been a miracle. And at the time, I desperately needed a miracle!

Armed with the Word of the Lord, I showed up in the gym five to six days a week. I went from 223 pounds to 175 pounds under the supervision of a doctor. The day that I was able to purchase my first pair of jeans at Dress Barn in size 13/14 is seared in my mind forever.

I could not stop praising God. "Thank you, Jesus. You are a wonderful God. You are faithful to your Word. Glory be to your name."

The joy of the Lord was all over me. It caused me to sing, shout, and skip for joy. I continued to show up on the treadmill with great expectations. After a time I was even able to do a light jog. That was an astonishment! My knees did not hurt, and my legs were stronger.

After one miracle, another one happened. I went down to a size 11/12, then to a 9/10.

Then something happened. Menopause. It came in like a thief in the night. It threw everything off!

For me menopause represented total resistance. My body went into a tailspin. No matter how much I exercised, I could not lose weight. No matter how much I reduced my eating, I could not lose weight. I even began to gain weight. Every drop of sugar caused me to store fat. I was at a loss. I was filled with horror.

I finally had several tests done and discovered I was insulin resistant. The nutritionist told me, "Your body is not absorbing the nutrients from your food because it is discarding what it needs and keeping what it doesn't need."

I left her office confused and defeated. The report from my doctor was as bad as that of the endocrinologist. Negative reports were swirling all around me. Then I heard a soft voice inside my spirit, "Whom will you believe?"

The Holy Spirit tried to remind me that the only report I'm to believe is the one that comes from God. Although the evidence was stacked on the side of the medical profession, I was to believe God. My scale even testified to the fact that what the doctors said was valid. However, the word spoken by the Holy Spirit caused me to wonder if their reports were actually true.

Just as in the parable of the sower (Matthew 13:7), the word God had given me was choked out by desperation.

For the next couple months I tried diet after diet. My body did respond to all of them, and I lost several pounds, but then I gained them back after a few weeks. Fear set in. I needed to get a word from the Lord.

I decided to write down exactly what I wanted from God concerning my weight. "Holy Spirit, I'm tired of struggling with my weight. Why is it that my weight keeps going up? What is it I am supposed to do?"

Conviction hit. The Holy Spirit began to speak: "You have not kept my word before you. You have listened to everyone else. You have placed another word in front of you."

The Holy Spirit reminded me as only He could about the word He had given me in the gym a few years earlier. I was to keep His word before me.

As I meditated on this, I began to understand this is what Christ did. Jesus endured the cross for the joy that was set before Him (Hebrews 12:2). The Holy Spirit had given me the word of the Lord so that I would endure the test and trial of menopause. He knew that my weight would be adversely affected by it; therefore, He supplied me with what I needed to remain committed to seeing God's word fulfilled in my life.

Impatience, desperation, and self-reliance had crept in when I was not looking. I fell to my knees and repented. "Oh, Lord, forgive me for going off course and for believing the report of others over the established word of the Lord."

As I was praying, the enemy caused a number to flash before my eyes: 180. He wanted me to establish this number as my new weight goal.

"I will not establish this as my goal in the name of Jesus. The Lord said 150. This prize is firmly set before me. I will hold on to this number and no other."

As I remained in the Lord's presence, I began to see myself slimmer, healthier, and at 150 pounds.

The Lord then began to teach me. Walking on the treadmill represented my progression in life. Although it may look like I am remaining in the same spot, I am not. I am advancing, and I will be able to move to higher levels because I will become stronger.

The treadmill also outlines the straight course I am to follow. This is symbolic of my spiritual walk in the Lord. "Your word is a lamp to guide my feet and a light for my path" (Psalm 119:105). He gave me His word so I would not be ensnared in darkness. He provided His word for me because the path He was taking me along I could not comprehend or see (Isaiah 42:16). God expected me to do one thing completely—obey.

As I obey daily, ritualistically, and faithfully, I will indeed trample the enemy under my feet. God himself will establish my weight loss as I continue to operate in faith, believing.

I had it all mixed up and twisted. The next day as I stepped on the scale, I was not filled with dread. I was excited because

I knew that something had happened. The scale read 188.0, the next 186.2, and the next 185.4. The Holy Spirit had established the direction my weight was to go in, and what He required of me was faithful obedience, not in what I see but what I know by the Spirit of God, who does not lie (Numbers 23:19).

One hundred and fifty pounds is my weight destination. I will not achieve it by my strength nor by my power, but by the Spirit of the Lord (Zechariah 4:6). The Holy Spirit lovingly reminded me that "all who are led by the Spirit of God are children of God" (Romans 8:14).

Lies That Kill

RITA A. SCHULTE

L ies. We hear them. We internalize them. We buy into them. The real problem comes when we breathe them into our souls and *believe* them, allowing them to form a cancer that eventually overtakes our being.

I know all about lies. I know the havoc they can wreak because I've experienced it firsthand. Lies killed my husband. They caused him to take his life in November 2013.

Mike was my high school sweetheart. We had been together for forty-two years. We had the normal ups and downs, disappointments, and sorrows most people experience, but if you asked anyone who knew us, we had what most people only dream of. I adored him. He was a successful dentist with a thriving practice; I stayed home and raised our children.

Mike was a Type-A personality. He was superman to everyone who knew him, especially to me. But superman forgot to tend to his own heart and the fragmented parts of his life. Those disappointments and losses he didn't process correctly got buried in his subconscious for far too long. Early in 2013, he started becoming paranoid. He was always untrusting of others, cautious and protective, but his behavior was becoming increasingly erratic.

In August of 2013 we took a trip with my son and his wife to Arizona. We quickly realized things were getting out of control. Mike was worried about people sabotaging his office. He thought people were planted at the restaurants we went to so they could watch him, and he was convinced the government was out to get him and put him in jail. It was bad. On several occasions he even accused me of being part of the conspiracy against him.

When we came home from our trip, things began to unravel quickly. I begged him to get help. He was prescribed medicine for depression and anxiety, and I learned later that he never took it.

One night I came home from work and thought Mike was asleep. I was working in the sunroom when I heard a gunshot in the field. I ran through the house and outside, screaming his name. No answer. Our son drove up on his motorcycle, and then Mike came walking down from the field to the driveway with the gun in his hand. I was hysterical.

A couple weeks later he kissed me good-bye in the morning and never showed up for work. His office was worried because he didn't come in. I called my son, and we drove to the airport where he kept his airplane. I was sure he would be there. I was so filled with terror I couldn't feel any sensation in my arms.

After a long ordeal, we finally got someone to come and open the hangar. My son walked in and finally called to me that his dad was in there and was okay. Mike had locked himself in the hangar and was sitting inside his car. It was at least 110 degrees in there, and he had been there for hours.

I ran inside, collapsing to the ground, holding Mike's legs and crying hysterically. When I stood up and looked at him, it was as if no one was there. He was blank, just staring into space.

We got him in the car and I immediately called his psychiatrist. They said to take him to the hospital, which we did. By then, he was fine. Laughing and joking. He told me not to say anything about suicide because he was afraid for his practice.

Like a fool, I initially complied. Later, we met with a social worker and I told the entire story. They prescribed some medication for him and we left.

There were several more incidents where he attempted to shoot himself. Every time he was late or wouldn't show up somewhere, I was hysterical. The torment never stopped.

One night he told me that it was hard to kill yourself. He pulled a gun out, and as we sat in bed, he put it to his side and told me how he watched the bullet go into the chamber (on this particular gun you could actually see the bullet in there). I cried and begged him to stop. I told him he was terrifying me.

None of us really believed he would take his life. Not even his psychiatrist. One night while we were lying in bed, he told me that he could never really kill himself because he couldn't leave me, and he wouldn't ever want to leave me with such a mess. My mistake was to believe him.

We went to our home in Florida with some friends. He was very sick and was scheduled to go to the Meier Clinic in Dallas. He never made it. He flew home a day ahead of me, and sometime between late Monday night after we got off the phone and Tuesday afternoon when I came home, he had shot himself. I found him in our bed.

Trauma asks us to put words to that which is unspeakable. For me, life became a living nightmare of grief, guilt, flashbacks, and reliving the unspeakable event at any given moment. The survivor takes on all the psychological baggage of their loved one.

As a therapist, I knew what needed to be done. I immediately got into therapy for trauma work. I joined three grief and suicide groups, and I had tremendous support from family and friends.

Still, I wanted to die. I believed I couldn't survive without Mike. The only one who could change that belief was Christ.

I had to be willing to walk head-on into this agony. There was no avoiding it if I wanted to move forward. I did things like getting back to sleeping in our bedroom alone (someone slept with me for the first couple months). The bedroom had to be renovated, the drywall and carpet replaced.

About two months after Mike's death, I was left alone in the house for about an hour. I sat outside the closed door of our room, rocking back and forth with my Bible in hand. God gave me this word: "My grace is sufficient for thee, for my strength is made perfect in weakness" (2 Corinthians 12:9 KJV).

Before I knew it, I was in the room, lying on the floor sobbing—but I was delivered!

Through my trauma work, I had some amazing visions of Jesus holding me. I saw Jesus and me in a boat with a storm raging around us (the storm representing the tormenting thoughts), when Jesus held up His hand against them as if to say, "Stop!" He held me tightly under His cloak to protect me.

The first vision that God gave me to replace the horror of what I walked into that afternoon in our bedroom was supernatural.

It was a huge wooden cross on the bed in front of Mike, and Jesus hovering above him with His hands outstretched.

Jesus' blood was pouring out over Mike. It became His blood I saw and not Mike's. It was for Mike's salvation. He let me know that in spite of the horror of that moment, Mike was with Him. That was powerful!

Next came my nephew's prayer. Jon was very close to Mike and wanted assurance from the Lord that Mike was with Him. Jon was going hunting with his dad, but that night he couldn't sleep, so he prayed and woke up early. He asked the Lord to give him a sign that Mike was in His arms.

Jon got up, still praying, and heard the Lord tell him which rifle to take and where to go hunting that morning. Jon specifically prayed that God would give him a 10- or 12-point buck as a sign. For twenty-five years they had hunted on that property but had never seen a buck that size.

When Jon got to his spot, he began questioning what God had told him about going to a different spot and using a different gun than he was used to.

A few minutes later, Jon noticed some rustling in the bushes. He fired. When he ran to see what it was, he found a 10-point buck! He called his dad on the walkie-talkie and told him what had happened. My brother-in-law, George, said he had been up praying for the exact same thing!

The movie *The Lion, the Witch and the Wardrobe* has always been a favorite for me. I am especially drawn to Aslan, the Lion representing Christ. God used Aslan to heal me in the most supernatural way of all during my trauma work. He appeared in one of my first visions, rearing up on his hind legs and roaring in the bedroom in response to the suicide. He was in a rage at the enemy.

After that vision, God had that lion appearing everywhere for me: on magazine covers, on TV, in movies, on buildings. It seemed everywhere I looked I would see Aslan and feel comfort.

The real freedom came in one of my last sessions with my therapist where I once again had to relive the trauma for her. This time, I was to take Aslan with me into the house, up the stairs, down the hallway, and into our bedroom, holding on to his mane.

As I recalled the event, I was able to reflect on the fact that Jesus, in the form of the lion, was not only with me, but also sensitive to my pain and horror in that moment. Before, I had only thought of how horrible it was for Mike in those last lonely hours or moments. Now I could enlarge my capacity to embrace my own pain and despair. I even found room to forgive myself for not returning home with Mike that fateful day.

Journaling about my journey gave me the opportunity to integrate my right/left brain as well as being able to evaluate the toxic thoughts and write out the truth with scriptural counter-statements. Through my personal therapy work, group work, focused reflection, reframing, and other components, I was able to change my underlying neuronal networks (thought pathways damaged by trauma), and begin building new healthy thoughts.

Each time a toxic thought came into my mind, I had to take it captive. This wasn't a quick fix; it has taken almost three years because of the nature of the loss and trauma. But now when I have a flashback, my brain defaults to the images Jesus gave me, and I have greater emotion regulation. There are new neuropathways now created by the very hand of God!

While my earthly story with my beloved has ended tragically, I know my eternal story with Him will never end, and when we are reunited again there will be no more tears, only unspeakable joy.

Three Friendly Strangers

DAYLE ALLEN SHOCKLEY

In October of 1998, I was preparing to teach at a ladies conference on the East Coast. The invitation had come a year earlier. Had I known that by the fall of 1998 I would be emotionally and spiritually bankrupt, I would not have accepted. But a promise is a promise, and I intended to keep this one. Besides, the hostess of the event was my dear friend. Not only did I need to go, I *wanted* to go.

On the night before I flew out of Houston, I penned a simple prayer in my journal: *Lord, be my strength. I am at my weakest.*

The next day I was the last unfortunate soul to board the packed plane headed for Baltimore. The only seat left was the first seat that actually faces backward, forcing you to sit there staring at the folks in the first row.

Across from me sat several ladies who seemed to be on top of the world—laughing and joking with each other between sharing what appeared to be a giant chocolate bar.

Of all places to sit, Lord, I thought to myself, *why here? I really wanted a bit more privacy. I practically have an audience already. Way to go, God.*

Sinking down into my seat, I felt all eyes on me. Nodding in their direction, managing a hint of a smile, I stuck my head in the book I'd brought, hoping the happy gals would leave me alone.

My sour attitude surprised me. It even upset me. It wasn't like me to be so unfriendly. I'm a Southern gal, and I enjoy talking, but today the idea of chatting with strangers sounded agonizing.

So much for my prayer for strength. I sensed it would take every ounce of strength just to get through this flight, let alone the weekend. *Way to go, God.*

Soon we were airborne. Just about the time the plane leveled out, the lady in the middle seat leaned forward and said, "Are you from Houston or Baltimore?"

Oh, boy. Hardly off the ground and already a question for me. *Does she not see that I'm reading?* Forcing a smile, I looked up and said, "I'm from Houston," hoping that would end the conversation.

It didn't.

"Well, I'm Janie, and this is my mom," she said, pointing to an elderly woman. I smiled at her mom, who was wearing the biggest diamond ring I'd ever laid eyes on.

Janie wasn't finished. "And this here is our friend." She pointed to the woman by the window who smiled and nodded my way. "We're all from Austin, going to visit friends in D.C., and we are so excited!"

"Well, that sounds like fun," I said, forcing another smile. "I really hope you enjoy your weekend."

"Thank you," she said, and leaned forward again. "Now, what did you say you were going to Baltimore for?"

I didn't recall saying, but I suppose that was her polite way of asking.

"I'm teaching at a conference this weekend," I said, knowing there would be a follow-up question.

"How interesting. And what are you teaching about?" There it was.

"I'm teaching a class about writing for publication," I said, wishing for a parachute at this point.

"No kidding?" Her eyes widened. "You're a *writer*?"

I don't know what it is about that word that sends folks into orbit, but mention that you're a writer and they often flip out on you. They must envision you sitting home all day eating bonbons, pecking away at the keyboard, ideas popping into your head effortlessly while waiting on your next big royalty check. If only they understood the struggles of this business. If only they understood how much labor is involved in writing well.

"Yes, ma'am, I'm a writer. Nobody famous, though," I said with a laugh.

"Oh my!" she said, clearly intrigued. "That is so *interesting*! A *writer*," she whispered dramatically. "Well, what kinds of things do you write?"

By this time, I must admit, Janie's charms were starting to grow on me a little, so I just went with it, going with the flow.

"Oh," I said, "I write articles for magazines, newspapers. I've written a couple of books. . . ."

She was instantly transported. "You've written *books*? Oh, my goodness! What are the titles?"

I shared the titles of my books, which were only two in 1998, and that's when her jaw dropped. She leaned way forward and said, "What was that first title?"

I repeated it. *"Whispers From Heaven."* Her jaw dropped yet again, then she touched my knee and fairly squealed, "Girl, I have that book!"

Without meaning to, I laughed out loud.

"No, ma'am," I said, thinking how adorable she really was. "I'm quite sure you don't have my book."

There was no way a perfect stranger from Austin, sitting across from me on a plane bound for Baltimore, would have my book, so I repeated myself. "I am sure it isn't the same book; there are other books with that title. But it's a nice thought, that you would have my book."

She wasn't listening. "Does it have a stained-glass window on the cover?"

"Well, yes, it does, but . . ."

"What is your last name?"

"Shockley, but . . ."

Turning to her mother, she beamed. "Mother, you know that book we've read several times? The one with the pretty cover that looks like a stained-glass window?" Her mom was nodding enthusiastically, her diamond blinding me. "Well, this lady right here—" She reached over and patted my hand. "This lady wrote that book!"

Covering her mouth, the elderly woman gasped and said, "Really? Oh, my goodness!" She stared at me and smiled. "I can't believe it," she said. "I just can't believe it. We love that book. I sure wish we had it with us so you could autograph it."

Since they'd perfectly described the book's cover, I had to believe them, but I was even more stunned than they were.

111

"Whoa," I said, still in a bit of shock. "Are you *sure* it's my book?"

They nodded in unison.

Suddenly we seemed like old friends talking across a dinner table.

I remembered the prayer I'd written in my journal—prayer for strength. And I'd been certain that God would answer by allowing me to have a quiet, peaceful, uninterrupted flight so I could gather my bearings and meditate.

But now it all made perfect sense. I knew why He guided me to this awkward seat and to these three friendly strangers. God knew that there's no better way to strengthen a despondent writer than to place her in the company of readers who find something remotely meaningful in her words.

When the conversation lagged, I leaned back in my seat and marveled at what had just occurred. I realized how often I questioned God in times past, and I wondered how many times I may have missed the answer to my prayer because of what I thought the answer would look like.

By the time the plane landed, I was ready to share what little I knew about writing with those who showed up for the workshop. I wanted them to know that writing well is hard work, getting published even harder. I wanted them to understand that there might come a day when they feel empty and out of steam, a day when they want to throw in the towel and quit.

But keep the faith, I would tell them, because their second wind would come. And sometimes it would come from the most unlikely people, in the most improbable places.

Way to go, God!

From Fantasies to Faith

VICKI DAVIDSON

Tears blurred my vision as I merged onto the highway. I was on the final stretch of the drive to see my therapist after weeks of missed appointments and excuses. My thoughts were a tangled mess, and I was consumed by guilt and shame. More than once, I was tempted to turn the steering wheel toward a path of no return, but I could not bear the thought of causing pain to my husband and four children. The promise of hope kept me in my lane. Deep down, I knew God had a plan, and I prayed He would give me courage.

When I arrived at the office, I could not speak, as tears continued to wet my checks. My therapist sat patiently, but it soon became obvious we would have no conversation that day.

"Vicki, I think you need more help than I can give. I'd like to recommend a ten-day outpatient treatment program at a psychiatric hospital. You will have classes and therapy sessions, and at the end of each day you can return home. I know you have a supportive family; they will be an integral part of your recovery."

I knew the time had come. I had to get out of my bed, get out of the house, and get the help I needed. But my mind was filled with doubts about my ability to persevere. I struggled to trust God and knew I would be tested. My recovery depended on allowing God to renew my mind, which was filled with questions. Did I really need this drastic, intense treatment? Would my broken relationship with God be further damaged as I faced my past? Was I at risk of losing myself? Would I be referred to as "crazy" for the rest of my life?

The journey began when I was a youth. I experienced occasional depression, and my mood swings were exhausting. They were exaggerated by undiagnosed post-traumatic stress disorder (PTSD) resulting from childhood sexual abuse. When the abuse began, I didn't understand what was happening. As I entered adolescence, I realized my abuser was taking advantage of my innocence, but I felt as if I had nowhere to turn. I began to retreat into a private world I created in my mind as a way to cope.

I was introverted and awkward in social settings, but when I escaped to that secret place, I was outgoing and sophisticated. In my fantasies I didn't have difficulty relating to boys. I created love stories and romantic encounters. I was beautiful, graceful, and desirable. It is no wonder I was increasingly drawn to that world.

The abuse stopped in my early teens when my abuser moved. Things continued to improve after I left home after high school. I married my college sweetheart shortly before turning twenty-one, and my fantasies began to lessen as I enjoyed the taste of true love.

My husband and I knew God had brought us together, and we were committed to a lifelong marriage. But soon, like most newlyweds, we realized marriage would be harder than we had expected. I began to struggle with intermittent depression again and possessed a poor self-image, which strained our relationship. I began to turn back to the comforting fantasy world.

For many years, I was able to hide my secret obsession. But by the time my husband and I approached our twentieth anniversary, the fantasies had escalated until they threatened to break into the real world.

In my mind, friendships with men would eventually result in an intimate relationship. Isn't that what had happened when I was a child? The man who had abused me was a family friend. I looked up to him as an older brother, but he expected more from our relationship than simple friendship. Why would I think it would be different with other men?

My marriage was deteriorating to the point that, in fits of anger and tears, my husband or I often threatened to leave. Our children became adept at staying out of our way, but also became increasingly bold at telling us to stop fighting. This was heartbreaking and sometimes forced a temporary truce. Inevitably, though, my depression and secret sin came back with a vengeance. My husband's pain and confusion erupted in anger. Inside the walls of our home, our family was in turmoil.

It's amazing that we were somehow able to hide our problems. To the outside world, we had a model Christian marriage. We attended Bible studies, served in ministry, and were recognized as active leaders in our church. I was a stay-at-home mom, only working part time and temporarily as needed to contribute to our family income. We did our best to raise our children in a Christian home. But it was getting harder to conceal what was happening.

Finally, my severe depression reached its lowest point. I quit working and spent most of my time cuddling with my pillow under the covers. I believed I was protecting my husband from a broken wife. I banished myself to the bedroom in an attempt to save my children from a mother they didn't deserve. At times, I was able to push through my desire to stay in bed to attend my kids' activities or fulfill my dwindling number of commitments. But once I arrived home, I headed straight for the couch in front of the television or retreated to the solitude of my room.

This became my routine for most of the summer and early fall. I couldn't see any way out. Despair continued to grow, and my mind was flooded with negative thoughts.

One life-changing day in early October, I was in my bed, covers over my head, crying over a recent sinful act that I considered unforgivable. My fantasies had finally overpowered my will, and I had approached a man about forming a romantic relationship. Thankfully, he refused. This man was actually a member of our church and married to an acquaintance of mine. He compassionately suggested I seek help.

Looking back at that situation, I believe God protected me from greater sin by bringing this particular man into my life. In His wisdom, God knew this encounter would open my eyes to the severity of my problems.

I confessed to my husband and asked for his forgiveness. It was devastating to hear him say he needed time to recover from his pain. I was ashamed and could not bring myself to turn to the Lord since I had fallen so far. I had welcomed Jesus into my heart as a child, and I should have known better. How could I have betrayed my family and my God?

After this, the days locked away in my bedroom began to blend together until, on a day like many others, something happened. Seemingly without warning, the Holy Spirit began to move. A tiny hint of hope filled my heart as I heard a still, small voice reminding me I was loved and had access to God's forgiveness.

I could almost feel the angels surrounding me and pulling me from my bed and onto the floor. I found myself on my knees, sobbing and filled with remorse. I was also filled with awe that God had revealed so lovingly and tenderly that He had not given up on me.

A few days later, I took that God-ordained drive to my therapist's office. The next morning, my husband accompanied me to the psychiatric hospital. I began the ten-day program that afternoon. After I completed the program, I spent several years in therapy and participated in a Christian support group.

Each day I grew stronger. Even though it took some time, with God's love carrying me along, my fantasy world was replaced with a faith and trust in the Lord that was greater than I had ever known.

Mental health professionals, family members, and many others played an important role in my recovery, but God's powerful healing saved me. God supernaturally used the secular psychological tools I learned to move me forward. He guided me through the recovery material in a way that kept me focused on His face in every class and therapy session. I began reading the Bible again and reached out to a small circle of friends for prayer and encouragement.

As part of my recovery plan, at the urging of the Holy Spirit, I entered seminary and earned a master's degree in Bible and theology. I began to write, not just for fun or in my journal, but for the purpose of teaching God's Word and encouraging others to persevere. I led a support group for depression and anxiety and was recognized as the go-to person at my church when someone needed confidential emotional support. I had never felt so blessed. I had never felt so close to my Savior.

Today, fourteen years after walking through the doors of the trauma unit, I clearly see how God used the events in my life to draw me into a deeper relationship with Him. Because of His grace, forgiveness, and promise of eternal victory, I found relief from the demons that had tempted and tortured me.

God restored me to a life of freedom. I am free from the fantasy world and sinful obsessions. Free to enjoy the blessing of family without dwelling on my past mistakes. Free to minister to other Christians who find themselves in situations similar to what I endured.

I know our all-powerful God performs amazing miracles every day. I know He performed a miracle in my life during those ten days of treatment and the years that followed. The broken woman filled with shame and regret is long gone. My marriage is solid and our adult children are serving the Lord in unique ways. I am still a sinner and face temptations, but I now stand firm in God's grace, confident of His forgiveness, and resting in the knowledge that He will never leave me.

I love to share my story of how God miraculously restored me. He renewed my mind and replaced my fantasies with faith.

Rebuking the Rain

JEANIE JACOBSON

B alanced precariously on our suburban home's roof, I clutched the dripping paintbrush and forced my quivering arm to keep moving.

Our tallest ladder hadn't reached the house's peak, so I'd climbed onto the attached garage's protruding roof. The grainy asphalt shingles felt unstable underfoot, but I only had a few feet of siding left to paint.

My husband, Jake, worked below me. He'd undergone multiple operations in the previous few years, and his joint replacements hindered his ladder-climbing abilities.

Jake tapped the ladder to get my attention. "Honey, you need to climb down. A storm is moving in."

Sure enough, a menacing gray cloud mass hovered overhead. I'd been so focused on painting the house I hadn't noticed the encroaching squall.

My internal alarm sirens blared. "It can't rain. It'll wash all the wet paint off our siding."

"There's nothing we can do about it," Jake said, clearing away paint supplies. "Come on down. You don't want to be up there if lightning hits."

A fat, storm-scented raindrop splatted against my arm. I groaned and sent up a halfhearted prayer.

"Lord, please hold back the rain. We can't afford to buy more paint."

A second raindrop hit, and I reminded God, "And my legs don't have the oomph to keep climbing on roofs."

Another taunting drop tapped my arm. I shook my head in frustration and noticed the tall extension ladder propped nearby. Seeing it brought to mind God's miraculous intervention when I'd painted our house years before.

The Lord had rescued me from a horrific fall from that very ladder in 1991.

I'd been on the top rung, about twenty feet off the ground, on tiptoe to reach the last unpainted inch of eave.

And I felt the ladder swing backwards.

I'd dropped the paintbrush and grabbed for the ladder, but it was too late. It continued its backward arc with me clinging to it. Toppling backward, tipped at a 45-degree angle, I'd cried out, "Jesus!"

Immediately, what felt like an enormous hand stopped my fall. It covered my back from waist to shoulder blades. For a moment I hung there, supported by the huge hand. Then it pushed me, still clinging to the ladder, gently back against the house.

I'd leaned my head against the wood siding while the hand held me secure. Once my trembling eased, the hand disappeared.

I'd climbed down the rungs and noticed the fence behind me. Had I fallen from that position on the ladder, the trajectory would have impaled me on the uncapped post below.

The ringing telephone below jolted me back to the present. While Jake answered, I chastised myself.

God had performed a mighty miracle for me back then. Where was my faith in Him now?

I prayed, "Lord, I'm trusting you to stop this rain. Please make it pass by without washing away the paint."

Another raindrop hit my arm.

"Please, Lord," I whispered.

Questions swirled through my mind. Would God stop the rain? He knew our time and budget restraints. If it rained now, we'd have to wait until the following year to repaint.

A clear Holy Spirit direction cut through my tumultuous thoughts. "Rebuke the rain."

I pictured Jesus in the boat rebuking the storm, but come on, that was JESUS.

"Is this really you, Lord?" I asked, "Because I don't think I heard you right."

A Bible verse immediately rose to mind. "I tell you the truth, anyone who believes in me will do the same works I have done, and even greater works, because I am going to be with the Father" (John 14:12).

And that posed a problem, because lately I hadn't been going to the Father.

Back in 1991, when God prevented the terrible ladder accident, I'd been a new Christian. I devoured His Word. I couldn't wait to commune with Him in intimate prayer.

But lately I'd become lax in my relationship with the Lord.

I still prayed daily, read my Bible, and attended worship services. But my fire had burned low.

In my mind, it made sense for the Lord to rescue me when I focused totally on Him. But why would He intervene now when I failed to give Him my best?

I peered down from the roof. Maybe Jake would join me in prayer. But he still chatted on the phone with his elderly father.

Again I felt a Holy Spirit nudge. "Rebuke the rain."

Even at this second prompting, I hesitated.

In the middle of the neighborhood, once again twenty feet above the ground, I sheepishly looked around.

What would my neighbors think if they saw me praying on the roof?

The Lord spoke once again, His spirit reverberating firmly within mine. "I told you what to do. Will you obey?"

Somehow I knew I'd heard the Lord's last direction on the matter. It was decision time.

Which concerned me more: how people perceived me or my obedience to God?

I straightened, feet straddling the roof peak, and lifted my right hand toward the sky. "Rain, in the name of Jesus, I rebuke you, and command you to stop falling. You will not touch this house until the paint dries."

I waited for a grand intervention, like a special effect from a 1950s Hollywood Bible epic.

While I didn't feel a supernatural power surge, I also didn't feel any more raindrops.

Arm still outstretched, I stood on the roof peak and repeated, "Rain, I rebuke you, and command you not to fall on this house."

Overhead the threatening downpour remained locked in the lead-colored sky. Jake walked out of the garage below me, phone in hand. His relieved voice floated up. "Hey, Dad, the rain completely stopped here."

An intense flood of gratitude left me shaky. I raised both arms to the sky. "Thank you, Jesus. Thank you, Lord."

God prevented the rain from falling on our home and held it off until the paint dried. Then a downpour began.

God's supernatural intervention that day reenergized my relationship with Him. He opened my eyes to the truth.

When I'd moved away from Him, He'd stayed close to me.

When I was faithless, He remained faithful.

When I put Him on the back burner, His love for me still burned hot.

That day I realized I didn't have to do everything perfectly. Yes, God desired close communion with me, but He didn't discount me for not being perfect. It wasn't about how good I'd been but how great He is.

Now when God directs me to do something out of my comfort zone I can obey, knowing I operate in His power, not my own.

At times storms arise in my life and threaten to wash away the plans God sets before me. Thanks to His grace, I can stand firm and walk boldly in the revelation the Lord used to set me free: I don't have to be perfect, because He is.

The Shepherd's Crook

KELLY WILSON MIZE

un! The voice in my head gently commanded. *Trust the Shepherd.*

The urgency of the moment jolted me into full focus. I never thought this would *ever* happen on my watch. Years of training, testing, and previous job experience should have prepared me for such an occasion, but I still couldn't fathom it. Sure, it was always a possibility; it was the main objective of my job. But regardless of whether I could believe it or not, it was happening.

A man was drowning, and I was the only lifeguard on duty.

It was a typical slow weeknight. The indoor pool was in the basement of the athletic facility at the small university where I was a student. To get to my lifeguarding job I only had to walk across the street from my dorm. The location was convenient, and my usually uneventful work consisted mostly of watching expert swimmers as they swam laps or families with young children sporting colorful floatation devices that helped ensure their safety. It was a part-time job that I often referred to as the best and "easiest in the world."

As a teenager I had been a lifeguard in my small hometown, and had recently passed a refresher course and completed the required CPR training for this job at my college pool. I had always loved the title *Lifeguard* and the idea it represented. But at the same time, I was never confident about my fitness level or ability to actually *guard* anyone's life.

The skills tests in the pool were never easy for me. Treading water with a ten-pound brick and retrieving "victims" from the bottom of the pool took every bit of strength I could muster. I passed, but I had to work harder than most, and I experienced much anxiety along the way.

On that particular day, an adult paraplegic man in a wheelchair and his elderly mother, neither of whom I had ever seen before, entered the pool area. The mother must have seen me looking at them with caution because she came over and assured me that her son, even though in a wheelchair, had extremely strong arms and was an excellent swimmer.

"He's a fish in the water," the mother explained with a chuckle. "Don't you worry about this one."

So I didn't. I smiled with relief at her reassurance, knowing people with limited strength in one part of their bodies were often extra strong in others. I had often heard that wheelchair-bound people could indeed be very good swimmers.

Still, I watched carefully as the man wheeled his chair to the edge of the deepest part of the pool and boldly plunged headfirst into the blue water. I waited anxiously for what seemed a very long time for him to resurface. He did, but his movements were weak and he struggled to keep himself afloat. His arms began to flail. I saw a look of panic on his face, and in my heart I felt a sickening wave of dread.

He needed to be rescued, and I was the only one there to do it.

God, what should I do? I prayed frantically, fully realizing that I didn't have a millisecond to lose. At that time, I was a senior in college and about 110 pounds. This man was much heavier. I knew I had to act quickly.

Run! Trust the Shepherd.

In that flash of divine inspiration, I remembered the shepherd's crook. As the name implies, the shepherd's crook is a long metal pole with a curved end designed to "hook" a struggling swimmer and drag him back to safety. The human-sized lifesaving tool is much like the actual staff a shepherd uses to pull his sheep back into the flock when they are in danger.

Because of the man's size, and mine, I felt the shepherd's crook was my only hope. More important, it was *his* only hope.

Obediently I ran, as the voice had commanded, skidding along the wet pool deck toward the wall where the shepherd's crook was hanging. The strong, familiar aroma of chlorine in the pool area began to sting my eyes, especially as it mixed with my own tears of terror. But amid the blur, I saw the surreal scene playing out before me in what seemed like slow motion.

I made it to the wall, grabbed the shepherd's crook, and struggled to where the man was, my bare feet smacking the damp concrete in a rhythm of urgency. It took several tries, but I was eventually able to wedge the hook under his arms and around his torso, pull him to the edge of the pool, and somehow (through strength that was not my own) pull him out of the water.

The chaos continued. As I dragged the man out of the water, he cut his foot on the pool ladder and began to bleed profusely into the water and then onto the pool deck.

I raced to find the first aid kit. Returning to his side, I clumsily bandaged the cut and ever so slowly began to breathe again. Ultimately, but sloppily, the three of us (the man's mother, the man, and I) were able to get him safely back into his wheelchair.

Thankfully, the cut turned out to be minor, despite the amount of blood, and the man appeared to have swallowed very little water in the pool. No call to 9-1-1 was needed, and no accident form was completed.

As I began to clean up the bloody pool deck, the man's mother thanked me and apologized for trying to convince me that her son was an expert swimmer. The two then left the pool abruptly. I can't honestly say that I was sad to see them go. It had been one of the most unsettling evenings of my young life.

After my shift, I crossed the street a little shakily, eager to relay the story to my roommate. But only later did the magnitude of that experience become completely clear to me: I saved someone's life. I didn't receive a medal or any recognition, but I saved the life of another human being. . . . Or did I?

The answer came quickly: I didn't save anyone. God did.

I had been a Christian most of my life and knew all about the love and miraculous power of God. But lately, He had seemed so far away. My faith had become inconsistent, and my witness was immature and ineffective at best.

As I continued to analyze the experience, I remembered the biblical story of Peter sinking into the water when he tried to walk on it.

> But Jesus spoke to them at once. "Don't be afraid," he said. "Take courage. I am here."
> Then Peter called to him, "Lord, if it's really you, tell me to come to you, walking on the water."

"Yes, come," Jesus said.

So Peter went over the side of the boat and walked on the water toward Jesus. But when he saw the strong wind and the waves, he was terrified and began to sink. "Save me, Lord!" he shouted.

Matthew 14:27–30

And of course Jesus chose to save Peter! But unlike the man at the pool, Peter wasn't sinking because his body was weak; he was sinking because his *faith* was weak.

What about me? It seemed I had been struggling to keep my head above water in every aspect of my life: school, relationships, and (for that night at least) my job! The Good Shepherd had laid down His life to save *me*, no crook needed. Was my faith strong enough to truly trust Him?

Miracles happen all around us every day: in homes, in churches, in hotel rooms, in the city, in the wilderness, in swimming pools, and in people's hearts. Every saved life is a miracle, but every saved *soul* is an even greater one.

You could argue that no miracle actually took place in the pool that day. A young lifeguard simply did the job she was trained and paid to do.

But I know the truth. God was with me, and just like the Bible promises, *His* presence gave me the strength I needed to pull that man from the water. In fact, at least three miracles took place that day:

1. A man's physical life was saved.

2. An insecure young woman experienced the personal presence of the God of the universe.

3. She was made aware, like never before, of *His* power in her life.

128

My career as a lifeguard ended not long after that. I soon graduated from college, got married, and left that "easy" job behind. But for my remaining days on duty, I was much more confident in my ability to handle any situation. Not because of my own adequacy, but because of God's. With the help of a lifesaving shepherd's crook, I had been reminded of the miraculous strength of the Shepherd working through me. He is the only one who truly has the power to save. Not just once, but over and over again.

God's presence in my life that day changed my perspective forever. I knew that no matter what obstacles I would encounter in the future, my all-powerful Creator would be with me. I could hear His voice and count on Him to miraculously guard both my life and soul.

Double Betrayal, Double Blessing

JULIE ANN LONDON

I popped awake at 2:28 a.m., stumbled out of bed, and headed up the stairs. Why was I going, and what was awaiting me there? I didn't know.

From the top step, as if led by an invisible cord, I turned and walked through the hallway into an office. I stepped across to the desk, reached behind it, lifted up a briefcase, and pulled out an envelope from its back pocket. Rather odd. It was from my longtime friend Camille, addressed to my husband, Tony.

For years, Camille and I had been like sisters. Before my family had moved away to another state, she and her husband, David, had been two of our closest friends. Our foursome worked a side business together, attended the same church, and spent time in each other's homes. Our families had traveled and enjoyed holidays together.

What could she possibly be sending him? News about the kids, or the business, or mutual friends?

I slid the five-page letter out of its envelope and began reading. Within seconds, a red-hot flush came over me as ugly words jumped off the page, words revealing their two-year affair—my good friend and my husband of twenty-eight years. How could this be?

Each handwritten page spilled over with emotion and passion—expressions of her deep love for Tony, sordid details of their numerous trysts, and what their secret romance had meant to her. She wrote how glad she had been that their traveling jobs made it all possible and that nobody knew.

But . . . they did know. She began telling of her husband's discovery, the embarrassing and incriminating evidence from a private investigator's tapes, how "hellish" life had become in their home, how their children—

I could read no further through the tears and dropped the letter to the floor. Nausea swept over me, and I doubled over in pain, struggling for the next breath, quivering uncontrollably, as if I'd been wrapped in a blanket of ice.

Shock. Disbelief. *How could they?* And how could I have been so blind, so naïve, so unsuspecting?

Double betrayal. How does a person ever forgive such a thing?

Everything in me wanted to lash out, to confront the wrong. But I was taught early in life to be gracious, never the confronter, ever the peacekeeper.

It had rarely served me well; on the contrary, it often took its toll. Every time I reigned dutifully as Queen of Denial, stuffing my feelings and avoiding conflict at all cost, it proved to be more harmful than helpful. Instead of setting healthy boundaries, I ran from them. Rather than allowing my emotions a healthy outlet, and expressing them honestly and openly, I'd opt to send them underground, where they silently, ceaselessly smoldered.

And that's what I did in the days following the devastating discovery. I kept everything carefully locked inside—the fears, the tears, the humiliation, and the hurts.

Surprisingly, as crushed as my wife-heart was, even more unbearable was the anguish over what my friend, the other woman, had done. How could she? We were friends! I never wanted to see her again.

Before long, I was painfully aware that animosity and resentment had wrapped their monstrous tentacles around my wounded soul and held me captive. I wanted to be free. But how?

Only God knew the depths of hostility brewing inside my mind and heart. And He loved me too much to let it continue. He had a plan, one that would soon change my life.

That plan unfolded one afternoon in the form of a surprise event. I call it "The Intervention." Mutual friends arranged for both of us women to show up at their house at the same time, totally unaware. David was with them. They ushered us down to their basement den and closed the door, leaving the two of us alone to face each other.

There we stood, neither of us daring to look at the other. Finally, as I raised my eyes to look into hers, and she into mine, something happened. Something I can only describe as *supernatural*.

In that split second before our eyes met, it was as if the Lord instantly removed my mind and my heart and replaced them with His. For the first time since the discovery, I looked at her—not with eyes of hatred and hurt, but with *His* eyes of love and compassion, and forgiveness.

A miracle, pure and simple.

She spoke first. "I never thought you could even look at me again, much less smile at me like that. I've never seen you so . . . so radiant!"

She was seeing the radiance of Jesus in me. I felt it, too, as if pure joy were oozing out of every pore—I couldn't have stopped it if I'd tried. How could I explain this extraordinary, supernatural love I suddenly had for her? I hardly understood it myself.

"To be honest," I said at last, "anything you see on my face is what the Lord has just put there. My heart can't love like this, but His can."

I reached out and wrapped her in a hug. She hugged back. We both cried.

"Jesus loves you, my friend. And so do I," I whispered in her ear as we embraced. Those nine words came naturally, refreshingly, to my soul, and for the first time in way too long, I was at peace with my friend, and myself—and the Lord.

As we sat down and continued talking, I saw in her a desperate need for hope and healing. Silently praying for the right words, I began encouraging her about her marriage.

"You two have something really special. You both want it to work. It will take time and commitment and a willingness to forgive. Most of all, it will take both of you getting back with the Lord and His Word." I smiled and leaned closer. "You can do it—He will help you."

She nodded and smiled back. In that instant, I witnessed a miraculous change in her, too, as though an enormous weight had been lifted. Indeed, it had, for us both.

We talked some more, heart to heart, friend to friend, much like we had before, but on a new, deeper level now. I don't know how long we were down there, but I sensed God's loving presence, and His pleasure, the entire time.

When at last we emerged from the basement, David and our friends were upstairs to greet us, wondering what could possibly be happening down there all that time. Had we done each other in, like the Gingham Dog and Calico Cat?

The moment Camille saw her husband, a grin spread across her face. She went over, put her arm in his, and said, "Honey, I think we're going to make it."

And they did, as they began their journey back to God, and as they let Him do the same kind of supernatural work in their hearts that He had done in mine that day.

In the months to follow, our two families' lives took different turns and faced some tough challenges. As Camille and David continued to seek the Lord and the truths of His Word, their marriage relationship grew, and by God's grace, it weathered the storm of infidelity—all the way through "till death do us part."

Tragically, ours did not. There were other women, ones I did not know, whose eyes I could not look into with the love of Jesus and the promise of His hope. Eventually, one of them replaced me as wife, and another replaced her soon thereafter. Life is messy. But God is good.

I learned that "replacement" has a positive side to it, as well. God's beauty replaced my brokenness. His strength replaced my weakness. His joy and peace replaced the ravages of war being waged in my soul. The enemy seeks to devour and destroy. The Lord seeks to rebuild and restore.

Yes, I've had moments of sadness that our thirty-two-year marriage and precious little family did not survive; and yes, I've had painful reminders of those dark days. But when these moments come, I choose to replace the negatives with positives, beginning with a grateful spirit. God did a miracle and allowed me the privilege of living it—a highlight of my forty-plus years of walking with Christ. For that, I am forever grateful.

And as traumatic as that middle-of-the-night discovery was, I am truly thankful for it: thankful that God led me to find that letter and face the harsh truth . . . thankful that He carried me through and healed my heart of the bitterness and grief . . . thankful that He demonstrated His love and power by bringing me safely out on the other side—a new creature, with my mustard-seed faith not only intact but multiplied a hundredfold.

Above all, I will always be grateful for the blessing—the *double blessing*—of experiencing His unconditional love firsthand, and then of having it flow through me to another soul desperately in need of it.

Ah, the beauty and freedom that await us if we're open to His "heart surgery," a supernatural work that is infinitely better than anything our human heart could try to muster up.

We are not stuck with our own negative thoughts and fragile emotions.

In an instant, He can wipe them away and give us the mind and heart of Christ.

No matter what we face, we can rest in His promise and the apostle Paul's words:

Each time he said, "My grace is all you need. My power works best in weakness." So now I am glad to boast about my weaknesses, so that the power of Christ can work through me. That's why I take pleasure in my weaknesses, and in the insults, hardships, persecutions, and troubles that I suffer for Christ. For when I am weak, then I am strong.

2 Corinthians 12:9–10

We need never wonder if He is enough, or if His strength can cover our weakness, or if we will survive whatever threatens to undo us. He is. And it can. And we will. To Him be all the glory and praise!

The Indigo Vessel

ELIZABETH GARRETT

I will never forget her words. "God has given you this weekend to help you through what's getting ready to happen," a conference speaker said.

Three days of focusing on my relationship with God had emptied my heart of past hurts and regrets, filling me with hope. I had been to the mountaintop.

How could someone suggest my darkest valley may be my next stop? I hoped she simply meant I might have a rough week at work.

At the time, internal conflict consumed my workplace, and I concentrated on outcomes to cope with the turmoil. Each conflict drove me further away from the rest of the team. My performance was at an all-time high, yet my relationships with team members could not have been worse. I saw no other alternative but to resign my position of five years.

Despite many accomplishments I'd had during my twenty-five-year career, I declared myself a complete failure and vowed never to work in my profession again. On top of that, my father had just died, and our nation's economy had plunged.

Weeks later, my husband's employer closed its doors. We opened our own business, and, during our first week, my husband was involved in a near-fatal car accident as an undetected tornado came out of nowhere and lifted his vehicle hundreds of feet away. The accident totaled both cars involved, but thankfully, no one was harmed.

Over the next few months, the business became profitable and demanded less of my time. I accepted a job managing a healthcare facility, fully expecting it to last into retirement.

Around-the-clock demands, physical plant challenges, employee issues, and other problems immediately began taking their toll. With the encouragement of my supervisor, I pressed on until I became a shell of my former self. Family members and friends begged me to quit, but I wasn't ready. I finally relinquished control after battling a chain of insurmountable obstacles. I found myself at square one all over again.

Shortly afterward, I dreamed someone spoke to me on God's behalf. He showed me a beautiful earthen vessel with a dark indigo finish and soft, translucent glaze. I commented on the vase's beauty, and I sensed God saying the vessel was me.

Scripture refers to God as the potter and us the clay. To become a beautiful or useful piece of pottery, the lump of clay is first spun on a wheel as slow, steady applications of water bring it to malleable consistency and strength.

The potter then carefully molds the vessel to avoid breaks. Water is incorporated as needed. His hands press inward, which forces the clay to climb upward. The most intense pressure is applied along the base. Then at just the right time, the potter pokes a hole in the center while constantly adding and releasing pressure as needed. If the vessel experiences too much pressure, then another—unwanted—hole will occur.

Then follows the shaping, drying, and trimming processes to obtain the weight and strength for the vessel to endure many hours of firing in the hot kiln. Once cooled, it undergoes a quick dust-removing bath, followed by the initial glazing. The potter uses the wire cutter to remove excess glaze, and then back into the blazing kiln it goes for twice the length of time.

This analogy ignited vision and hope within me. Contrary to a beautiful vessel, I saw myself as a big, cracked pot riddled with holes. Throughout my life, I had concentrated on *my* to-do list. I was achievement-oriented rather than relationship-friendly. As a career woman, my job title and salary defined my self-worth.

Now, according to God's messenger, I was being transformed into something not just beautiful, but exquisite. I couldn't help but wonder how such a transformation could occur when strong-holds of unworthiness, abandonment, and condemnation consumed me. Yet God had taken the time to have someone tell me, through my dream, how all my messes were being molded into a stunning work of art. He pointed out how each hardship, stress mark, and challenge was a reason why the vase would be so beautiful.

Shortly after the dream, a minister friend suggested I take a few months off, if I had that luxury, to discover who I was in Christ. This seemed strange because I knew I was a child of God and a faithful Christian leader. Quite honestly, though, I couldn't even grasp what she meant.

Instead of pursuing the discovery quest with all my heart, I did so halfheartedly and kept praying for God to send me the job of my dreams. I just knew the right title and income would cure all my woes. Interestingly enough, I was offered a slew of jobs, but each one came with a major drawback.

I clearly understood God saying He could give me a job, but that wasn't what I needed. A perfectionist and go-getter, I kept being asked to volunteer for demanding jobs in ministry. My busy, over-extended life—even though dedicated to God—had left my heart empty. I was busy doing as much, if not more, as I had done when I worked. Now I wasn't even getting paid for it.

Self-doubt gripped me and triggered feelings of unworthiness no matter what I did. I began hearing voices threaten to force me into eternal condemnation. My thoughts obsessed on battling demonic whispers. Crippled by fear, I got so I could hardly leave the house. God still had my heart, but the devil fought relentlessly to destroy my hope. My indigo vessel had become all but a faint and distant dream.

At wit's end one December, my husband and I approached the guest pastor at church. He had counseled numerous college students battling similar challenges and knew exactly where I could get the counseling I needed. During the next year, I was diagnosed with obsessive disorder, similar to postpartum depression, except mine was targeted toward God.

Could it be that my mother's death when I was a toddler and the ensuing abuse triggered in me an unknown anger toward God? I had always overachieved in every area possible and been "Little Miss Perfect," never breaking a rule. The thought of being mad at anyone, much less God, horrified me.

As the counseling helped me walk through the doors to the past and open unhealed wounds, the spiritual warfare ravaged. One night around midnight, I was pouring my heart out to the Lord, asking forgiveness for demonic thoughts, which continued even while I prayed. It seemed as though an evil person had encamped in my home and chattered nonstop in my ear.

I sat down to read the Bible and opened it to a psalm I never remember reading even though I've read the Bible through several times. My eyes focused on the words, "You have rescued me from the depths of hell" (Psalm 86:13 GW).

The Holy Spirit directed me toward John 3:17: "God sent his Son into the world not to judge the world, but to save the world through him."

He spoke directly to my heart. I knew He had not abandoned me. Although I felt forgotten and condemned, He was directly telling me He rescued me, saved me, and loved me. Would I ever truly believe it?

As each day passed, I continued to counsel, meditate on Scripture, enjoy Christian fellowship, and call on trusted friends when desperate for prayer. By the time the most intense part of this experience was over, I knew all of my friends' schedules so extensively I would know who to call at any given moment when battling the enemy.

Thanks to Scripture, prayer, and medication, the voices in my head quieted down, and I slowly began to heal. My internal conflict and soul searching opened opportunities to become closer to friends with similar backgrounds. Instead of saying yes to every volunteer opportunity, I've become selective and use my talents where they can be most effective. Plus, spending time with family is finally a priority.

Perhaps the most amazing part of the transformation is that I'm no longer a perfectionist who has an anxious intensity in each breath. I've become a relaxed, joyful person who embraces each moment and whose shell has been completely broken.

Clearly God answered my prayer of breaking strongholds. Little did I know how agonizing the process would be, but like the indigo vessel in my dream, I want to be worthy of serving my intended purpose.

I even look forward to the final glaze.

The Tiniest Angel

INGRID SHELTON

My husband had recently passed away. Now I was alone with my thoughts and my grief. I knew I would never see him again this side of heaven. We had always wanted to leave this earth together. But now I was left behind. Alone!

"Come with me to a retreat," a friend invited me. "You need to get out, get on with your life."

I hesitated. *Go without my husband? My best friend? It would be too painful.*

I was just too discouraged to do any traveling because joy had eluded me since the first day of my widowhood. But now I did nothing much except stare at the four walls around me. Perhaps being among people might ease my pain.

Getting ready for the five-hour drive, I took my little suitcase, my bag, and my water bottle to the car in the garage. Just the day before I had cleaned my Toyota and vacuumed the inside. Now as I put my water bottle into the small compartment between the two front seats, I felt something hard and very small. I was astonished to find a tiny wooden angel there.

I gazed at it in wonder. Where did it come from? It had not been there the night before when I had wiped that compartment clean. Throughout the night my car sat in a secured garage. And I was sure that the windows had been rolled up tight, so no one could have tossed it inside.

Now, as I gently cradled this tiny wooden angel in my hand, I didn't want to take the time to go to my third-floor condo to leave it there. Quickly, I put the angel back into the compartment beside my water bottle. I would take it up to my condo on my return.

As I drove toward my destination, I thought about the past, when my husband and I had traveled together, stopping at gift shops, looking for angel figures. It had been fun to browse through the selection of angel memorabilia in various towns.

Bittersweet memories surfaced of our years traveling together, but now I was alone with only memories of that time.

I loved angels. Throughout the years I had collected a large cabinet full of angels of all sizes and shapes, but I had never seen an angel as small as the one I had found in the car. On various occasions my husband had surprised me with some unusual angel figure. The angels always reminded me of eternity, where angelic hosts sing praises to God, so each year I decorate my Christmas tree with angel figures.

On my return home a week later, I parked my car in the garage again. Picking up my suitcase, my bag, and my water bottle, I took the elevator up to my home on the third floor. Entering my condo in the twilight, I put the suitcase and bag on the floor in the hallway and my water bottle on the small glass table beside the front door. Then, as I headed into the kitchen to turn on the light, I almost stepped on something. I bent down to pick up what I assumed was some garbage to deposit in the trash bin.

To my shock and amazement, I had picked up a little blue wooden angel. Turning on the light to examine the angel I now held in my hand, I was stunned. Was it the same angel I had found in my car before I had left? With my heart pounding, I raced down all three flights of stairs to the garage. The tiny angel was not in the compartment, nor anywhere else in the car.

Yet I knew I had left that little blue angel in the car throughout the trip. And I was sure there was no way I could have brought it up, even accidentally. It could not have stuck to my stainless steel water bottle. No magnet was attached to it. Besides, the water bottle was still sitting on the little table in the hallway.

Had I brought it up with my bag or suitcase? No, they were still on the floor in the hallway. And the angel could not have attached itself to my clothes unless the angel somehow jumped out of the compartment. That didn't make sense.

Then how did this little angel get from the car to my kitchen floor before I even entered the kitchen? I had no explanation. I kept thinking of all possible ways the angel could have come up, and I ruled out all of them. All except one—it could only have come up by supernatural power.

I had read in the Bible of angels appearing to men in human form. They could transform themselves into any form or size in their likeness. Had this tiny angel used his angelic power first to get into my car and then to appear on my kitchen floor where I could not miss it?

I slumped down into my husband's favorite armchair in the living room. Cradling this tiny angel in the palm of my hand, I suddenly noticed a tiny red figure attached to the angel's chest. No bigger than my thumbnail, a tiny person was held close to this little angel's heart. Did this tiny person represent me? And was this angel a reminder of my guardian angel?

I did not have an answer. I was in awe at the angelic power surrounding this event.

I vividly recalled my husband's last night on earth.

"Who will take care of you?" he had asked with concern in his eyes when he had realized he would no longer be able to look after me. I believe that this little angel was my husband's last gift to me as a reminder that I was never alone.

Today, my little blue angel is sitting on the small glass table by the front door. Every time I look at that tiny angel I experience a sudden surge of joy. "For the angel of the Lord is a guard; he surrounds and defends all who fear him." This verse from Psalm 34:7 often flashes through my mind. This tiny wooden angel is a constant reminder that God has appointed a guardian angel to protect and help me and to remind me of His constant love for me.

I am and never will be alone, even without my husband. And even better, this tiny blue angel is tangible proof that Jesus is with me and will never leave me.

A Society with Jesus

JAMES STUART BELL

The tangy salt breeze stirred my shoulder-length hair as I stood somewhat precariously with my Bible on a huge square boulder that was assaulted by waves of the Atlantic. Cape Ann in northeastern Massachusetts is a beautifully serene place that breathes peace and is ideal for spiritual retreats.

It was a warm late May afternoon after the semester ended, and I was convinced by a flamboyant Jesuit at my college to go on the spiritual exercises retreat of the founder of the Society of Jesus, Ignatius Loyola. So there we were, about twenty college kids that the priest had hand chosen for a five-day guided retreat of instruction, prayer, and silence amidst the sprawling grounds, endued with the serenity of wind, waves, and a multitude of rocks and trees.

This particular afternoon marked the third day of the exercises. Three weeks previous I had surrendered my life to God—sort of. When I told my Jesuit friend, he quickly included me on the retreat list. For a conservative Jesuit priest, he was an anomaly. He was of French extraction and went around campus in his priestly garb with cowboy boots and a cowboy hat. Many versions of the Bible have Jeremiah complaining, "Lord, you have deceived me" (Jeremiah 20:7 GW). But some versions translate the Hebrew as "seduced" (NJB), and so he would shout out in ecstasy with arms raised, "Yahweh, you have seduced me!" He was overwhelmed with God's loving pursuit of him.

Early that spring my closest friend had written to me and said he had become a Christian. We had been "witnessed to" by a self-proclaimed "Jesus Freak," and my friend accepted the bait and made the full commitment. In early May I reached my lowest point, imbibing radical politics, Eastern religion, and psychedelic drugs in search of the meaning of life and God. I reached out and asked the Holy Spirit to enter me. I experienced an immediate, wonderful experience of God's love and forgiveness, though I still hadn't read my Bible or understood all of its teaching.

So when I entered the hallowed halls of the retreat center, I was still somewhat of a crazy, mixed-up kid—spiritually. By now I knew that Jesus was the supreme head of the pantheon of gods, but I wasn't sure what that all meant. I had previously thought of Him as some sort of "reincarnated perfect master," and at least that absurd notion was gone.

A college friend entered that front door at the beginning of the retreat and whispered to me, "I wonder how Christ and Baba Ram Dass fit together, or do they?"

I had met the guru Ram Dass at a lecture a month earlier and had been a devotee and proselytizer in my college dorm where Steve and I lived even before that meeting. I told Steve I wasn't sure, but the retreat might tell the story.

Five days is a long time to contemplate your past and present spiritual state and your relationship to a God you need to know much better. The retreat for the Jesuits could extend as long as thirty days. But regardless of how many days, they were all considered "silent" retreats. You could speak to the spiritual director who gave talks around four times a day, but not to the other participants.

A lot of the students joked about how difficult that would be, but as we waded into the teaching, prayer, self-examination, liturgy, and communion, I could see by their intensity that the others, like me, were embarking on an inner journey with God.

After a deep, Christ-centered conversion, Ignatius Loyola, in the sixteenth century in Spain, developed spiritual exercises that were biblically centered, focusing on the life, death, and resurrection of Jesus. Our focus was to be one of self-surrender, or as I remember the expression so well, "docility to the Spirit" as we sought His will. There was a pattern that the participants (or disciples) would normally go through over the five days, but God dealt with each person uniquely, so the pattern wasn't the same for everyone. The two stages that most affected my life were Purgation and Illumination.

Each day between the meals and the teachings we would take our Bibles to a quiet spot and meditate on the previous teaching. How did it relate to our lives and our relationship to Jesus? The Purgation stage was a surprise to me. We were told it might be a difficult day. I thought I had confessed that I was a sinner a few weeks before and had been delivered. But as I opened my heart to God and we reviewed my life, He gently showed me a greater depth of sinful intention than I had previously known. As time progressed, the shame and guilt gave way to a deeper appreciation for God's ability to remain holy and yet excuse my sins because of Jesus Christ's payment. He would go to that extreme to get me back.

The highlight for me seemed to be the evenings when we would each return from our solitary paths in the chapels, out among the trees, or hiking on the rocks on the ocean's edge. Because of the enforced silence, we could only whisper things like "pass the bread," and the aura it created almost mesmerized me. I began to understand the importance of solitude and silence with the retreat participants together. Among a group setting of disciples with the same teaching, Holy Communion, and spiritual goals, the sound of silence was just astounding to me.

This was especially true after the last talk by the director after dinner. We had a lot to ruminate on, or as they call it, contemplate. Though it was late May, the coastal winds could bring a chill in the evenings. Our Jesuit would light a fire, and while some people went off to their rooms, many would stay huddled together on the couch with blankets, staring pensively into the crackling fire.

I glanced at a few faces, some with knowing smiles, others seeming to contend with a particular thought or issue. The silence was indeed "deafening" and so overwhelming that, ironically, it kept each one from distraction or having to act in a certain way.

It was a powerful moment of community. Though all were not committed to Christ, many were, and others were struggling but were along the way to that place. All I knew is that the Spirit of Christ was working powerfully on those fire-lit evenings, pursuing us passionately right where we were at on our journey. If we laypeople together weren't members of the Society of Jesus like the Jesuits, I felt that when we were together in quiet, we were, to coin a term, a society with Jesus.

On the day of Illumination it was as if I had been resurrected from the Purgation of my soul into the light of a new beginning. The gravestone had been rolled away into the light of ever day. I was beginning to get a glimpse of the whole picture that Scripture was presenting. I was beginning to feel challenged and confident that God had a place for me in the grand scheme of things. I felt uniquely loved and could look at the future with new hope because I was putting my life into His hands and was willing to trust Him with His plan, not my plan. (Although I actually didn't have my own plan as I began to wind up my college years.)

So there I stood on that immense rock slapped with bubbling surf, my big Bible flapping in my hands, scouring it in the bright afternoon sunlight.

God, what are you saying to me? I was realizing that it isn't enough to go through a "saving" experience. If you've experienced His personal love for you, then you have to follow Jesus wherever He goes. My eyes fell upon a verse in the book of Jeremiah: "I knew you before I formed you in your mother's womb. Before you were born I set you apart and appointed you as my prophet to the nations" (Jeremiah 1:5).

At that moment I was overcome with the grandeur of God, His wisdom and love past finding out. He planned for me not just in the womb, but also before it, and He had an exciting life in store. At that moment I moved into the role of disciple and accepted His lordship. I spoke aloud, "If you want me to be a prophet to the nations, I'll do it. But if you want me to clean bathrooms I'll do that, too."

I enjoyed a bit more of the mountaintop experiences over the next day or so, and suddenly it was time to go back into the world. As we filed out, I saw my friend Steve. I said quickly, "Jesus—absolutely. Baba Ram Dass—no way."

I don't know if he was convinced of my convictions, but I pray he was. As it turns out, I never became a prophet to the nations or even a pastor, as I later thought might happen. But I did become a husband, father, and grandfather, and am blessed by many other wonderful things. Though I have lost touch with all those spiritual seekers, I pray that each one finds, in their own way, what I found. For me it was a life-changing miracle, and the effects continue on to this day. Great is His faithfulness!

The Other Side of Forever

Swanee Ballman

After our last child graduated from college and moved out of state, my husband, Frank, completed chemo and was given the all-clear from non-Hodgkin's lymphoma. The Crohn's disease he had battled since he was nineteen had worsened even after two surgeries, but he still functioned quite well—the kids and I dubbed him the Energizer Bunny™. Yet when the company where he had worked for years downsized, he took an early retirement from his fast-paced and stressful position.

Free to relocate near our son, in 2007 we sold our Florida home and bought land in north Georgia. Frank drafted plans for our retirement home and planned to do much of the construction himself. We were both excited about this new stage of our lives.

Shortly after we poured the concrete foundation, though, Frank suffered severe pain. Tests showed that his intestines appeared to be knotted in numerous places. In a nearby city, we found a gastrointestinal specialist who felt he could alleviate some of Frank's issue through surgery. We were cautiously optimistic, since this wasn't Frank's first rodeo with surgery to remedy Crohn's symptoms.

During pre-surgery tests, we received shocking news: non-Hodgkin's lymphoma had returned. That meant an oncologist had to join Frank's medical team. Our retirement plans took an abrupt turn.

As we prayed the night before the surgery, the Lord led us to Isaiah 40:4: "Fill in the valleys, and level the mountains and hills. Straighten the curves, and smooth out the rough places." A still, small voice within me whispered, *The doctor will not be the surgeon. The Holy Spirit will.*

The Holy Spirit would perform the surgery? As believers, we clung to that promise.

After a six-hour surgery, the doctor approached me. I saw the fatigue in his eyes and in his gait, but his smile encouraged me.

"Frank's intestines were unbelievable," he said. "I have never seen such a twisted, gooey mess. But I was able to straighten them and remove the goo that had bound them. All looks smooth now."

Frank recovered quickly and soon resumed the house project, although chemo treatments held him back somewhat. But his determination to reach his goal far outweighed his health issues. Construction, which he initially expected to complete in a year, dragged on for three years. It consumed so much of his life that he wondered what he would do after we moved into the new house.

The Other Side of Forever

Once chemo treatments ended, Frank was placed on a harsh maintenance drug, which attacked his white blood cells with a vengeance. Twice after he received the IV dosage, he ended up in an ICU several days later. But our Energizer Bunny refused to stop. Often he would have his arm attached to an IV tube, connected to a tennis-ball-sized drug container, which he stuffed in his pants' pocket while he hammered.

After the drywall and carpet were installed, Frank finished the kitchen and one bathroom. With that much done, we received a certificate of occupancy from our county building department. What a blessing to finally sleep in our new house, even if it still needed lots of work. Frank was tired but eager to complete the other baths, and he began to arrange his man cave.

Three weeks after we moved in, Frank awakened me to say he felt really bad. We had gone through this routine twice before, so I packed the essentials and drove him to the hospital thirty minutes from home. When we entered the ER, his pain level was off the charts. By the time he was assigned to a room, he was begging for more pain meds.

That evening he was in an ICU bed. With his pain under control, he told me to go home to rest. I kissed him and dragged my body to the car for the lonely ride home in the dark.

I had just prepared for bed when the phone rang. An ICU doctor said Frank needed to be placed in a coma, but he wanted to see me first. I rushed back to the hospital, but when I arrived, he was already unconscious.

For the next eighteen days, I sat by his side and prayed. I clung to Psalm 91:16, "I will reward them with a long life and give them my salvation," because God had always brought him through. Why should this be any different?

Our daughter and younger son, both living in California, flew east the first week Frank was in the coma. We took turns staying overnight in the ICU waiting room.

One early morning as she slept on a couch, our daughter awakened. She felt her dad's presence hovering over her, but he wasn't there. A few minutes later a nurse told her Frank had suffered a heart attack and the medical team wasn't certain he would survive.

At home that same night, I felt Frank was with me. His presence seemed larger than life. I brushed off the sensation, but a few minutes later, in the early morning hours, my other son pulled into my driveway. Our daughter had called him about the heart attack, and he insisted on driving me to the hospital.

Frank survived that attack, but suffered another heart failure a few days later. The kids had returned to California, and I sat alone in the waiting room that night when the doctor told me. I paced, pleaded, and cried out to God. I quoted every Scripture concerning healing that my numbed brain could retrieve.

Again, Frank pulled through, but he was still in the coma with no signs of improvement. Daily dialysis and pumping fluid from his lungs offered no signs of improvement.

During his third week, a former patient with a similar medical history visited the ICU. Several nurses eagerly introduced us, and he shared his amazing story of how the Lord had healed him from what seemed a hopeless situation. I was convinced more than ever that God would do the same for Frank.

Toward the end of the third week, I met with Frank's medical team, who said they needed to stop their efforts to save his life. They removed all unnecessary IV fluids and ceased dialysis.

My sons were with me the next morning as we watched the body that no longer resembled Frank expire. The man I had lived with and loved for thirty-nine years was no longer with me.

Later I recalled the night when my daughter and I felt Frank's presence. We both believe that he stepped into eternity then, and what we saw lying in the ICU bed was merely his sixty-two-year-old flesh receiving artificial sustenance.

After the funeral passed and the kids returned to their lives, I felt an overbearing loneliness. The house Frank had almost finished meant nothing. I had no memories of him living in it.

I wasn't angry with God, but I was confused. Did His Word not promise to give me the desires of my heart? What had I missed? Where had my faith weakened? Were my prayers wrong?

I struggled for weeks. When I ate, I was alone. I would see older couples together and my heart would break over and over. We had planned to enjoy that kind of life together for many years beyond retirement. I shed many tears—in the car, at church, by myself at home. Sleep was out of the question. I was a mess.

One evening as I stood in the yard looking heavenward, I cried out, "You promised Frank long life. What happened? You promised!"

A peace covered me as that still, small voice spoke to my heart. *I've given him eternity. How much more life do you want for him?*

Immediately all was well with my soul. Frank was okay, and will always be okay. He didn't have to worry about what he would do after he finished the house. I'm sure God has given him something to do for a very long time!

I know Frank is in good hands. So am I. The Lord has blessed me with a new husband, and we have plans for a long life together. But whatever happens, I will someday experience the life that Frank has.

And that makes all the difference in how I live each day.

Finding Faith in a Foreign Land

VERONIQUE BENNETT

I had just left my grandmother's funeral in Tournai, Belgium. My spirit was in great torment. I had realized that at twenty-three, I knew very little about the profound issues of life and death. So, during the rituals of the church mass, I dedicated my life to find the answers—or die trying. What else truly mattered?

I went back to the attic in which I was living as an ascetic and locked myself inside for three days. The Eastern spiritual books that had fascinated me now seemed hollow. But a phrase that kept echoing in my mind haunted me: "Get up and walk!"

What was that supposed to mean? Being raised in a country as old as Belgium helped me to connect to the old Middle Age pilgrims. I thought maybe I would find the answers if I walked toward a country where the spiritual world was important, like India with all its gurus.

With my crude calculations, I figured that if I walked for about a year, I should reach its borders and be closer to the answers. The next day I was on my way, having written a letter to my mom to say good-bye and giving her instructions on what to do with my few possessions, just in case I didn't come back. I was the eighth child out of twelve, so she had plenty of others to keep her company.

I bought a map of France and decided that I would give my French-speaking culture one last chance to give me the answers. And, with this in mind, I left Belgium on that November morning and crossed over into France.

Three days later, as I arrived at a crossroads, I saw three huge crosses adorning the countryside. I had rejected Christ and His religion after hearing my dad deny the existence of God when my older brother passed away at age twenty-one. But there, startled at this common sight in Europe, I realized that I didn't know who Jesus was and why He died in such atrocious circumstances. It happened two thousand years ago. What could that have to do with me today?

Something unusual took place as I stared at those crosses. It was as if I had been wearing nothing but an old raggedy coat of prejudices, and all of a sudden it was ripped away from me, leaving me able to think and see Him in a new way.

Thoughts arose in my heart with something like a challenge: *If you are willing to go all the way to an unknown India, and you are honestly looking for answers, you must also open up your heart and mind to consider who this man was.*

After this strange encounter, at the end of my twenty- to thirty-mile journey each day, I would look for the church in the village. As I walked, I would ponder and admire the wonder of the landscape. It was so beautiful in its autumnal array, soothing to my soul, and yet the day was also so well ordered, just like a clock. There was morning, noon, and night without my having to lift a single finger to orchestrate it. Could it realistically have come from an enormous Big Bang? Didn't the clock have a clockmaker?

At the first village I came to, I hoped the parish priest would enlighten me. But no, when I told him I was looking for God, he just said bitterly, "I oversee a large parish and I know . . . no one is looking for God."

I left the next morning, still no closer to finding the answers to my questions: Was there a God or gods? Was there anything beyond this painful earth existence, or was death the end?

After traveling on foot for several weeks, I was getting rather disappointed about not meeting people who were more helpful in terms of spiritual answers. I decided that perhaps it would be better for me to just read the story of Jesus myself.

I went to a village called Lamarche (meaning "The walk"), and there I met a man at the town hall who let me stay at his house while he visited his sister. At his home, I found a Bible and spent most of the night reading the Gospel of Matthew. I could not stop. I had never owned a Bible or read it on my own. I was fascinated by the things Jesus said, like, "I am the light of the world," and "No one can come to the Father except through me" (John 8:12; 14:6).

I thought, *This guy is either a crazy lunatic and should be locked up, or he said it because it is the truth.*

The next day I discussed the Bible with the gentleman who had graciously let me stay at his house. He said he had read the Bible after his wife passed away, but had concluded it wasn't a reliable book. Again, I didn't seem to be any closer to finding anything of worth. Nevertheless, I challenged anyone who might possibly be out there: "If, invisible as you are, you exist, God, and Jesus is what He says He is—the *only* way to you, a *Father*—then I need some kind of proof. If not, I'll just burn the book and look elsewhere." I added in my desperate plea that it also had to be a proof that would be tangible to me. I wanted to meet people who were radical about their lives and beliefs. I meant people who "walk the talk."

I left the man's house on December 9. I was now more than 350 miles away from home and winter had settled in. I wrapped my full-length cape around me as I struggled against the pouring rain and the strong wind that whistled around me.

I stopped at a few farms to inquire about staying in the barn for the night, but my big, drenched black cape and bright orange hair must have given me a scary appearance, and three times my request was denied. The last farmer warned me about his big German shepherd dog he would loose on me if I didn't leave immediately. When I told him I was going to Rome to find God, he directed me to his Swedish neighbors, who were "always talking about God."

I left in the direction he had indicated and found a lovely home just a little farther down the road. Oh my! What was I to do? Just ring the bell of complete strangers? I felt like a beggar, but I was frozen to the bones, so I had to risk another rejection. When I saw their garage I thought I could ask them if I could stay there to get out of the storm.

This is how I met Orian and Anita Backrid. They looked a little surprised to see me when they opened the door, but they responded warmly when I gave them my "I'm looking for God, and I'm going to Rome" spiel.

161

Orian said, "Oh, you don't have to go anywhere to find God. The Bible explains how to do that. It's really quite simple. Come in and we'll show you."

Finally, it seemed I had found someone who "knew" how to find God. But what could be simple about that?

They invited me in, and around hot cups of coffee they opened the Bible to the passage about the Samaritan woman. As Orian spoke about Jesus' love for me, His sacrifice on the cross, and my need to be forgiven of my past and its wrong choices, I felt an overwhelming sense of grief and loss. Here I was with this lovely couple who knew nothing of me and yet they were taking me in, no questions asked.

I had thought I was messed up because of my parents, society, bad boyfriends, etc., but here, without them judging me, I felt convicted that I alone was responsible for the way I had wasted my life. Yet I felt such an intensity of love and acceptance coming my way that I could not help sobbing uncontrollably.

When Orian asked if I wanted to pray to give my life to Christ, I said yes. I knew the people back home would probably not understand and would no doubt reject me, but I also knew deep down that this was what I was looking for.

I didn't sleep in a barn or in their garage that night, but in a lovely guest room. The following morning I was welcomed with a delicious breakfast and an invitation to stay for as long as I needed to. Anita gave me a brand-new Bible and a warm embrace.

I stayed for about a month and even shared my best Christmas ever with my newfound Swedish friends. It was the very first time in my life I understood who was in the manger, the Divine Lord of all. I had received my sign and now I wanted to give my all to this amazing Savior. I was baptized by immersion on Christmas Day surrounded by the twenty or so Christians from this tiny church in the small village of Gray, near Dijon, France.

The amazing thing I later learned from the Backrids was that they were discouraged in their ministry the day I showed up. God had chosen a wayward young woman to walk all the way from Belgium to not only save her but also to encourage them!

What changed? Well, everything. I was and am in love with . . . yes, God. He has given me—a loner, lost and hate-filled—a new heart of forgiveness, a book to live by, and a family—the family of God, as well as my own. And He's given me a sense of destiny and a relationship with Him that will last into eternal life!

Mom's Terrifying Tumble

SHARON RENE DICK

W hen my mother took a fall, I had the feeling that God would have a lesson for me in the episode. "So, Lord, what are you trying to teach me?" I prayed as I sat in the emergency room waiting for my mother to return from getting a CT scan. Of course, I prayed for good test results, but I knew that God wanted to give me so much more.

This Saturday had started out like any other. I'm single, and my seventy-five-year-old mother lives with me. Our Saturdays usually consist of sleeping late, lounging around the house, doing laundry, and occasionally going out to eat with friends. Simple, peaceful, and easy.

But for me, life wasn't as peaceful as it appeared. I've always been a bit OCD and a worrier, but after my father passed away and Mom moved in with me, I became a real control freak.

Surely God needed my help running the universe. At least the part of the universe that I inhabited. I decided that if I checked the door locks multiple times, removed any obstacle my mother might trip over, made certain she took all of her medicine, and reminded her to keep the alarm on while I was at work, I would prevent bad things from happening.

Oh, I prayed, but I seemed to have more faith in my nervous rituals than in God's power. Sitting in the hospital, I realized how foolish I'd been.

The technician wheeled my mother back into the room, and I jumped to my feet to hover around the exam table while the nurse and technician helped Mom lie down.

"I'm all right," Mom said. "Didn't need to come to the hospital."

"You fell into a glass curio cabinet." I shook my head while my heart raced and my stomach churned.

The terrifying tumble had happened around noon. Mom had just taken a shower and gotten dressed. I was in her bedroom talking to her, and somehow she had tripped and fallen backward into our large glass cabinet. I felt like a participant in a horrible nightmare. Her elbow hit the glass, followed by her head. The glass shattered around her as she fell back into the shelves and our collection of trinkets.

Mom lay on the floor, her head and shoulders in the cabinet. A jagged slice of glass hung above her neck and large sparkling hunks surrounded her.

It was a miracle that I did not have a heart attack on the spot.

"Are you all right?" I asked, kneeling beside her.

"I don't know," she said, dazed from losing her battle with gravity.

I carefully moved the chunks of glass away from her body, getting a few nicks in the process, then helped her sit. She got to her feet, and I helped her to the bathroom so we could inspect the damage.

I could barely breathe. Blood poured from her elbow, and red drops trickled down her neck. I expected to see a huge gash in the back of her head. Her scalp was cut, but there was no large injury.

"I'll get my shoes on and we'll go to the emergency room."

Mom pressed a wet washcloth to her elbow. "I think I can doctor these cuts myself."

"You have a pacemaker and take a blood thinner. We're going to the hospital."

Later Mom told the nurse she hadn't wanted to come to the emergency room and didn't think she needed to be here.

"Oh no," the nurse said. "Anyone taking blood thinners needs a CT scan after a head injury."

Somehow I stopped myself from shouting, "See, I told you so!"

Thankfully, the CT scan gave us the all clear. The nurse patched Mom's torn elbow and sanitized her head wound. Amazingly, the cut didn't require stitches.

When we came home and looked at the shattered cabinet, I realized just how good God had been. Large jagged chunks of glass covered the floor and bottom of the curio. Smaller hunks lay scattered around, mixing with miniscule razor-sharp pieces.

Someone had been in control of Mom's fall, and it wasn't me. Only the hand of God could have shielded my mother from the splintered glass. Perhaps He had sent an angel to cover her body and keep her from harm.

"Your guardian angel is going to ask for a transfer," I said.

We laughed.

"I hope not." Mom hugged me. "He did a good job."

Then I realized what God wanted me to learn. Simply put, I am not God. All of my worrying couldn't change a thing, and I couldn't possibly have planned for and prevented every possible catastrophe. I'd never once considered that the curio might present a danger. Even if I had, I couldn't have moved it. The thing weighs a ton.

I was powerless to protect my mother that day. But God wasn't. He had no difficulty protecting Mom. He is the only one who can guard my friends, my family, and me.

I wish I could say that I've become a carefree, hang-loose kind of person, but that would be a lie. I still worry and fret more than I should. But I have learned that it's better to let go than to go crazy. Sometimes in His sovereignty God allows bad things to happen, but He never leaves us. He stays with us as we go through our sorrows and pains.

Now when I pray, I expect God to answer and handle things as He sees fit. I've confessed my flaws of doubt and fear. I've asked to be forgiven for foolishly believing that I am capable of controlling things. God has forgiven me like He always does. Relinquishing my need for control has brought me a sense of peace. I'm more relaxed and probably healthier. And Mom's certainly glad I've let up a bit.

Jesus said to "look at the lilies" (Matthew 6:28). They don't worry, spin, or toil, yet they bloom with the beauty of God's love. God is able to do far more than I could ever imagine. He is the only one in control.

In the Twinkle
of the Night Sky

ROBERTA UPDEGRAFF

I sat on the cinder-block wall and gazed at a million stars stretched across the Honduran sky.

It had been more than a week since I'd had word from my husband. He'd set out with two friends ten days earlier, driving a small school bus we had christened *La Pequeña Mula*— the little mule. The bus carried forty-plus sewing machines for a women's cooperative in Tegucigalpa, along with boxes of clothing and other necessities for survivors of Category 5 Hurricane Mitch.

"It's not my first rodeo," Mark had assured me when I expressed my concerns about the journey through Mexico, Guatemala, and Honduras. It would be his third trip to Honduras, though the other two had been by air. He also reminded me he had more than a million miles behind the wheel of a big rig.

He pointed to the words painted across the back of the bus: *We go with God.*

How could I argue with that?

He'd been so excited about making the trip, each obstacle in obtaining the customs clearance and permits had been a notch in his faith-belt of confidence. A trip down the Pan-American Highway would check off one of the quests on his bucket list—and "with a twist of mission," Mark had pointed out.

"I'm not much of a carpenter," he'd said of his accomplishments participating on work teams in preceding years. He wanted to donate his time using his talents—diesel mechanics and long-distance hauling. This trip would be just that! It was more than five thousand miles from Pennsylvania to Tegucigalpa.

Mark had recruited two friends—one was a Honduran pastor we had gotten to know on the previous trips, and the other was a Spanish speaker from Pennsylvania. While I organized the packing, Mark modified the bus to include hammocks for sleeping. Family and friends shared in the excitement of his "ultimate road trip."

We had been confident that he did, in fact, go with God.

But now? I sat alone with my trepidation—fear I dared not share with my children, who'd accompanied me ahead of him to Honduras, or the other team members.

I closed my eyes against the tears, pushing the recollection of our happy send-off party from my mind. I thought of my adult children, curled up in sleeping bags on the floor of the church where we had been camping out for the last week. The village had no electricity or indoor plumbing.

169

We'd come to a small Mayan village in the mountains of northern Honduras to help rebuild homes destroyed by the hurricane. Day after day we worked in mud up to our knees, wearing clothes saturated by the constant drizzle that preceded the nightly downpour.

All three of my children had signed up for this work trip, along with my oldest child's girlfriend. This was the first trip to Honduras for all but my youngest. I was the leader of our group of twelve; all but one other were newbies. And I was coming apart inside, afraid for the plight of my husband and his friends.

Night after night the rain on the leaky tin roof not only rattled my nerves, but also mocked my faith. I felt inadequate as a leader, crippled by my fear.

"I don't want to be afraid," I whispered.

I gazed into the indigo sky at stars as brilliant as the planetarium shows I'd enjoyed in college. I sniffled, brushed away the tears, and willed myself to be brave.

The words of "How Great Thou Art" came from deep within: "I see the stars . . ."

I praised from the expanse of my diaphragm, "How great thou art, how great thou art."

I continued into the next verse, accompanied by the streaks of a half dozen shooting stars. One hymn followed another until I contentedly rested in the peace that had enveloped me.

"You will see Mark the day after tomorrow," came the still, small voice on the evening breeze.

With a full measure of joyous trust, I tiptoed through the maze of slumbering team members. I wanted to wake my children but chose to hold my secret in my heart until morning.

I crawled into my sleeping bag on the dank, cold, cement floor. And with the surety of a parent's love, invisible hands pulled the cover to my chin and brushed tear-soaked tendrils from my forehead to plant a kiss. "Thank you," I whispered.

Over breakfast, to my chagrin, my children playfully rattled off jabs about my "out-of-key serenade" the night before. Doubt ambushed. Had I imagined that promise the night before?

My chest tightened at the team's curiosity about the insomnia that had led to my wee-hour serenade. I shared the words the Lord had told me, that I would see my husband the next day.

Soft chuckling reverberated around the makeshift breakfast table next to the smoky adobe hearth. I held back tears, my confidence in God's promise now shaken. After all, we were in the middle of nowhere serving in a mountain village off the beaten path, with the Pan-American Highway miles and miles away.

"We will see him tomorrow," I insisted. My youngest patted my arm.

The next day we headed out. We would go the Mayan ruins at Copan for a couple days of relaxation before returning to Tegucigalpa for our flight home. We would stop in the office of the Honduran Christian NGO with whom we were serving. Although the plan had been that Mark would go straight to Tegucigalpa (four hours south), I fully expected to see him at the office—grinning with success.

The next day when we stopped, I got word that my husband had called just hours earlier. He'd crossed the border into Honduras after having been detained in Mexico and Guatemala.

"He's safe!" I exclaimed to my children and the rest of the team when I climbed back on the bus. I hadn't gotten to talk to him, but my prayers had been answered, I assured them.

"Convenient," I heard someone whisper. "She changes the prayer to match reality. Didn't God tell her she would see her husband?"

I burrowed into the seat and willed myself to nap as we headed on toward Copan a few hours northwest.

"La Pequeña Mula!" The voice of my daughter, rows in front of me, startled me.

The bus slowed.

My son was in the aisle. "It's Dad!"

The bus riders were filled with excitement as we coasted to a stop at the side of the road. Before the driver could pull the door lever, I was in the door well.

The little yellow school bus slowed and maneuvered to an opening on the other side of the road.

My team poured out of the bus, my children directly behind me.

Mark stepped out of the bus, grinning.

I ran and leaped into his arms before he could get his bearings. In John Wayne fashion, he said, "Hit a few snags."

Snags? My husband's faith confidently carried him through several precarious encounters. He joked about the "tips" (bribes they'd had to pay at several makeshift roadblocks). Their overnights at small hotels came with security guards wielding sawed-off shotguns.

We gathered in a circle on the roadside near the two buses. I closed my eyes, leaning into the reassuring Presence who had abided with all of us—even me in my darkest doubts. Mark's faith, the two Spanish-speaking co-pilots, and prayer had carried them five thousand miles.

After sending the team on to Copan with my co-leader, I boarded *La Pequeña Mula*. My relaxation would be in the arms of my beloved after we delivered the bus and its contents to the NGO headquarters near Tegucigalpa. The team would join us in the capital city in a couple of days.

As we headed toward our destination, the travel-weary trio bounced around plans for another Pan American road trip the next year. It seemed I was the only one who'd hit a faith snag. My stoic but true partner kept his faith close to his chest.

I joked that there would be no second trip, but deep down, I knew this was just a maiden voyage for Mark. I felt the twinkle in the Lord's eye for this hands-on guy of few words.

My God Can Do Anything

KAREN WINGATE

Most women consider mammograms a yearly annoyance, an obligatory test to endure. I decided to make a party out of my checkup, so I invited a chorus of friends to catch up with each other's lives in the waiting room while I surrendered myself to the cold slab of the X-ray machine. We finished the yearly tryst with a visit to our favorite fast-food restaurant.

Three days after my mammogram, an ophthalmologist discovered that a torn retina in my left eye needed repair, and scheduled surgery for two weeks later. His technician told me to wipe my calendar clean for several weeks after the surgery. In a rush to get as much done beforehand, my husband and I carefully orchestrated a host of errands on his day off. En route to the car, I stopped by the mailbox and retrieved the dreaded letter telling me I needed to have another mammogram.

I threw it on the table and snatched up my purse. "I don't have time for this."

My husband said, "Take the letter with you. We'll stop by the doctor's office while we're out. We'll do what we need to do."

Several stops and a flurry of phone calls landed me an appointment for the retake the next day. I called Jule, one of my friends, for a ride and moral support. She would drop me off and visit her mother-in-law in the nearby care center, she said. She didn't mind the possibility that my exam might be a drawn-out affair.

"We'll take the films first and have you wait for the reading," the technician had explained on the phone the day before. "If they're positive, we'll do a sonogram. You're lucky the doctor who reads the films is in that day so you won't have to wait."

"It's nothing," I told Jule as she dropped me at the hospital entrance. "It was probably operator error. They just need a second look."

Assuring me she'd heard of other women who'd had the same dilemma at this facility, Jule drove off, leaving me alone for Round Two. The second mammogram went smoothly, reinforcing my belief that this was a waste of time. I went back to the private dressing room to wait.

Reality set in. What if the results were positive? Only weeks earlier, one of our church members had paraded through these same halls only to hear the dreaded word, *cancer*. Her surgery revealed cancer cells spread throughout her lymph nodes, beyond what the doctor could remove.

I had to be practical about this. I had to be ready for such a diagnosis. It could happen.

I placed my head in my hands. Cancer in addition to a torn retina? While the results of the mammogram would probably be negative, I had legitimate cause for concern over my impending eye surgery. Legally blind since birth, I've dealt with eye issues throughout my life, starting with congenital cataracts. Doctors didn't know how to safely remove cataracts from the eyes of a baby, so a series of childhood surgeries left me with faded vision and damaged eyes. For years I've lived with the sobering truth that I was at high risk for several serious eye disorders and that my limited vision had an equally uncertain time frame.

The retina specialist said he might only be able to restore the recently lost vision or that my vision could end up worse than it already was. Knowing my visual history better than he did, I was well aware of the risks.

During the several months since Dr. Reddy first suspected my torn retina, I had struggled against discouragement. My façade of "I can conquer anything" slipped precariously on the thin ice of my deteriorating vision. My belief that God would provide and continue to use me in spite of more loss of vision was shaky at best. Some days I had more courage and acceptance than others. On darker days, discouragement doused me with "I can't" and "What if?"

After the doctor's decision to proceed with the retina surgery, I can honestly say I came to terms with the uncertainty of my future. God would take care of me; I had no doubt. No matter which way the surgery went, I was willing to trust God's best judgment for my life.

Now, sitting in that little dressing room, clutching my hospital gown that accentuated my vulnerability, the possibility of breast cancer rattled me. Wasn't there a statute of limitations on the number of crises a person could face at any given moment? How could I handle both cancer and vision loss? Could I? Could God?

I was too young to ponder my mortality, but I wondered if this was the beginning of the end of my life's productivity. Were my days of ministry over? Would my minister husband's flock have to take care of me instead of my taking care of them? Was I strong enough for this? There was so much more I wanted to do, so much I hadn't accomplished.

Determined to shake off the morose thoughts, I flipped open my tablet and checked my Facebook notifications. The top post announced a prayer meeting for my impending surgery organized by my Bible study group. This was the first I knew about the prayer meeting. A private message from my husband asked me to call him when I had a moment. I fished out my cell phone and punched his contact number. He wanted to tell me that a fellow minister had stopped by his office to rave over a recent article I had written for a magazine.

Overwhelmed by the two affirmations from God, I returned my phone to my purse. Then I heard a voice so strongly that I looked around the room for another person. The tiny room was filled with God's presence.

"I am not done with you yet."

My God was big, bigger than cancer, bigger than diminished eyesight. He could and would use me even if my life journey included both conditions. He could do anything—hadn't I said those very words to my Bible study ladies countless times? Was God calling me to live the very thing I had taught?

One of my favorite stories in the Bible is of Daniel's three friends who faced the ire of a king gone mad with power. Their God was able to deliver them, of that they were certain. "But even if he doesn't, we want to make it clear to you, Your Majesty, that we will never serve your gods or worship the gold statue you have set up," they told the king in Daniel 3:18.

Yes, God could remove cancer. He could restore my vision. But even if He did not, I could count on Him to carry me through. I would determine to trust Him no matter what happened. I would follow Him even if my body failed me.

Softer words entered my head. *It will be all right.* I relaxed in peace. Even if both prognoses were for the worst-case scenario, I would be all right.

A gentle knock sounded at the outer door, and I opened it to a smiling technician. "Your test was negative. You can get dressed and go home."

I was relieved but not surprised. It was, after all, what I expected. Operator error. Yet I walked away from the hospital moved by my encounter with a God who took the moment at a crossroads to assure me of His plans for my life.

I am not done with you yet. Time would prove God had a different interpretation of those words than I did.

A week later, I lay on the operating table. Much to my chagrin, the procedure was done under local anesthesia. If I had been given a sedative to give me a "twilight sleep," I didn't know it. At first I didn't appreciate the earful of operation room chatter, but in retrospect, I'm glad I was awake.

Two-thirds of the way into the surgery, Dr. Reddy said, "Mrs. Wingate, I'm usually cautious about predictions, but I think your vision will be better than it has ever been before." He explained that besides repairing the torn retina, he was cleaning a debris field of cataract remnants. That would widen my pupil, which had been decreased to pinpoint size by one of my bungled childhood surgeries.

Better? Was it possible? After surgery, I spent the first week facedown, the second week doing nothing, and the third week battling eye inflammation, elevated eye pressure, and irritating sutures. I made multiple trips to the doctor's office to face more needles, tweezers, and eye drops than I care to remember. Eager to see something, anything, I chafed at the doctor's prediction that it would take four to six months for my vision to optimize. Each week seemed like a year.

Throughout the difficult recovery, I clung to the doctor's words: *better than ever*. Could it be that God had planned this all along—that instead of expecting me to trust Him through the loss of my vision, I could wait patiently for the beautiful, extraordinary gift of improved vision? Only He could give better sight to a woman born blind who was now in her mid-fifties!

Finally, I was fitted with new glasses, and the doctor's prophecy came true. Throughout my childhood and adult life, my vision had been a dim 20/200. As I wrapped my new glasses around my face, I could see at an all-time new record of 20/80.

I could see stars in the sky, flowerpots on neighbor's porches, the texture of dirt in my garden, a hummingbird at a feeder on the other side of a window, and raindrops bouncing on the sidewalk! I could now participate in worship because I could see the PowerPoint slides from the sixth row of our church sanctuary. I could wave at friends halfway across a room and catch my husband's rolling eyeballs at my poor attempts at humor. The world was beautiful.

God truly was not done with me yet. He wanted to give me a second look at the world.

My Little Red Heart

JAN APILADO

The piercing ring of a phone jarred me awake. My heart pounded and my hands fumbled as I reached for the lamp switch and the phone. As I pressed the phone to my ear, I checked the clock. "Four a.m. This is not good."

"Hello."

"Sorry to wake you, Mrs. Apilado. This is Dr. Jacobs. I'm one of the chief surgeons here at the VA hospital. Now, don't panic, but your husband's infection is spreading and his condition is deteriorating. He's listed as critical. To save his life, we must amputate his leg."

As I struggled to breathe, I gasped. "Oh no, doctor! Do I have time to get there? It's more than an hour away."

"I'm sorry, Mrs. Apilado. We can*not* wait that long. He must get to surgery *now*!" he answered.

"Don't you need me to sign permission papers?"

"No, we had him sign them earlier while he was lucid. We did this just as a precaution, in case he didn't respond well to the antibiotics. But now surgery has become necessary."

"I'll be there as soon as I can," I answered.

"Well, be careful," he said. "I know you're upset, so drive safely."

As my mind struggled to process the full impact of the doctor's words, I saw everything around me, including myself, swirling into a dark pit of uncertainty. After a few deep breaths, I tried to absorb and gain some understanding of the doctor's words.

I then knelt down on our bedroom floor and went to the Lord. First, I asked Him for protection over my dear man, this mate He had given me forty-one years earlier. Next, I asked God to keep me calm and strong and enable me to handle whatever this day would bring, and to help me accept His will.

Ever so slowly I began to feel a sense of His peace and His presence. As His love held me and warmed me, my mind began to focus. Then I dressed and drove the fifty-some miles to the hospital.

Over the years, my husband, Corky, and I had discussed how blessed we felt to be living in God's plan. We shared in ministry to a small country church, where he was the pastor and I taught Sunday school and led our youth activities. Recently retired from our necessary money-making careers, we thoroughly enjoyed actively working for God.

For the first time in our lives, we could devote all our time and energies to serving Him, and He truly blessed our efforts. When we first accepted the pastor's position at this beautiful church, the average attendance for Sunday worship was eight to ten adults. We felt encouraged and grateful at how God had grown our congregation to thirty-five, with nearly a dozen young people and children.

Because many of our rural families heat with woodstoves, one of Corky's favorite ministries was to cut firewood for some of our neighbors and widows. He had purchased some trees the Bureau of Land Management had cut down for power line access. He and a friend spent a full day cutting and splitting the logs for his "wood for widows" ministry.

After he'd showered, he noticed that bark dust sifting into his boot had rubbed a small open sore on the back of his right ankle. After treating it, he saw his doctor the following day for a tetanus shot. The doctor took a look at the raw spot and said, "It looks fine. Keep doing what you're doing for it."

Five days later, Corky began to experience leg pain and swelling. The following day, which was a Sunday, some red streaks appeared and started to move slowly up his leg. By then, he could barely stand on that leg. I begged him to let me take him to the ER, but he adamantly refused to go until I preached his sermon for him.

"I just can't let our people down," he said. So I conceded, drove to church, preached the sermon he'd prepared, and requested prayers for him. Then I rushed home, packed a bag for him, and helped him into the car.

Upon our arrival, the ER staff immediately put him in a bed. Very quickly, doctors and nurses were attending to him and performing diagnostics. After the results from his blood work came back, the ER doctors ordered him to be admitted. They determined he needed a high-power course of antibiotics to fight a vicious streptococcal infection in his bloodstream.

Around nine that evening, I drove home. I fed myself and our Rottweiler, Sarah. Hoping for a good night's rest, I'd climbed into bed with both phones on my nightstand.

Now, as I waited in the surgical ward's waiting room, I held myself together fairly well while I phoned our four kids with the news about their dad. Then I called our three local churches, asking that they place Corky on their prayer chains.

After putting on a brave front over the phone, I fell apart again. His doctors had made no promises that he would survive the surgery or even the few days following surgery.

Finally, his surgeon came out and called me into a conference room.

"I'm sorry," he said. "We had to go above the knee. We had to be certain we got all the infection. It is a very fast-moving bacteria. For now it's touch and go for him. As we speak, he's being transferred to the ICU floor, so you can go there now and wait."

After Corky was settled into the ICU, I was finally allowed to see him. My eyes filled with tears as I looked down on my beloved. He looked so pale and small. My heart ached to see the empty space under his blankets where his leg had been. Oh, how I would miss watching him walk. It was one of the first endearing impressions that I'd loved about him. He had such an easy, relaxed stroll, yet it was always with purpose.

Then I began to count the needles. Ten IVs dripped fluids into the veins of his arms, wrists, and neck. His nurse, such a sweet lady, explained each IV to me and assured me that he would be her only patient. He would remain under her care for twelve hours each day, and her replacement would be assigned the same duty.

After she left me alone with him, I eased my tired body into the chair by his bed and prayed. For the following five days he remained in ICU. With each day his survival chances increased, so we began to breathe a sigh of thanks to the

Lord. On the sixth day, when he was stable, his doctors moved him to a regular room. On the seventh day, he underwent a second surgery to prepare the nerve and muscle needs for the final closure and the healing of his amputation. Through all of this, I knew I was coping only by God's strength and power.

On the evening after the second surgery, as I was soaking in the bath and began to wash my legs, I noticed a faint outline of a tiny red mark on the front of my right leg.

Hmm, I thought. *I've never noticed that before.*

Being so tired and emotionally drained, I simply dismissed it.

I visited my dear Corky every day for the next two weeks of his hospital stay. He was then transferred to a rehab center, which was more than a hundred miles away from home.

I leaned into the Lord more and more for wisdom and strength to keep our household running and to keep our home fires burning. This was in February, and we, too, heat our home with a wood-burning stove.

One evening, as I again soaked in the tub, I could not believe my eyes. There on my right leg, at the exact place where my dear man's right leg had been amputated, was a small, perfectly formed red heart. All the surrounding skin was clear and remains clear today. Is it possible that my capillaries had joined together to form this perfect heart? I don't really know, but I am certain that my wee red heart is God's gift to teach me and to remind me to regard my man with the same love and respect that I'd always held for him.

I realized He'd placed this on me to help me remain compassionate and understanding of my husband's special needs. The Lord knew I would see my special heart every morning as I dressed and every evening as I prepared for bed. What a wonderful way God created to keep me from feeling sorry for myself and to teach me to consider some of the challenges my dear husband must deal with every moment of every day.

Yes, our lives changed drastically on the day that his leg left us. Corky had always been the strong, decisive leader in our relationship and in our home. He was the man ever willing to put himself in harm's way to right any injustice he'd witnessed. Yet he was also tender, never neglecting to tell me how much he loved and appreciated me. With the loss of his leg he's had to give up much of his strong self-image. He was always our driver and protector. He was the planner and the adventurer, all combined with being a God-loving, Jesus-preaching pastor. Feeling unproductive has been his greatest struggle, since he also no longer pastors a church.

I view life with a new perspective now. I've learned there is a delicate balance between giving him my respect and support without mothering and smothering him during this great change in the dynamics of our relationship. I have had to become more patient, more confident, and not so timid about making decisions. God proved that He is in control, so my faith is deeper and more consistent in times of trouble.

One of our more difficult transitions has been to accept graciously when friends and neighbors offer their help. We had been accustomed to being the givers but had not learned to be the takers. Even today, we remain humbled by the generosity of our rural community. Volunteers from one of the churches delivered and stacked our entire winter's wood supply. A young man we'd known since elementary school posted an appeal for donations on his company's bulletin board. He presented us with nearly one thousand dollars cash when it was so desperately needed for gas money.

I now also must oversee all the upkeep of our home, our acreage, and our vehicles. God has taught me through the reminder of His little red heart on my leg that each day is His gift. It is a gift not to be taken for granted, but one to be treasured in the companionship of this man whom God chose for me.

Flowered Wallpaper

ROBERTA KAUTZ

*D*escending the stairs, I stared in confusion at people standing on ladders busily pasting ugly squares of olive-green flocked wallpaper to my dining room wall. When I reached the landing, I sank onto the bottom step. How had these people gotten into my house? What were they doing here, and who gave them permission to put this ugly wallpaper in my dining room? Sitting there, I knew that if they asked me what I wanted, I would have chosen flowers.

I woke with a start. Since seeking healing from the effects of growing up in a violent home, I'd been having dreams that gave me valuable insight about where I was in my healing journey. They were a gift from God, providing a visual of what my heart knew but had not yet found the words to express.

This dream clearly had significance, so I grabbed my journal and pen. I wrote everything I remembered, including the questions I had asked, and I prayed for insight. Then I sat quietly and waited.

In my mind's eye I saw that the ugly green paper covered about two-thirds of the wall. I remembered a workshop I'd recently attended that focused on examining our lives to see if we are doing what we are called to do, or if we are spending our days with activities we will someday regret.

The presenter had us graph what percentage of our lives had passed and what percentage we had left. I remembered my surprise when the graph showed that about two-thirds of my life was in the past. I also remembered the nagging feeling that I was ignoring what God was calling me to do and was not doing what I wanted to do with my life. I felt powerless as I walked out of that workshop.

For some time I'd sensed God calling me to quit my teaching job to stay home and develop my writing and public-speaking skills. God's prodding, which had started as a whisper, had become like a megaphone in my head. Up to this point in my life when I knew God was speaking to me, I quickly obeyed. So why couldn't I find the courage or words to tell my husband and others in my life what I believed God was calling me to do?

And what about the rest of my life? It didn't look anything like I wanted it to look. My days overflowed with responsibilities, leaving no room for the things I loved. I couldn't remember the last time I'd read a book for pleasure. Though I loved the ocean, it had been years since I'd spent a day with my feet buried in the sand, listening to the rhythm of the waves and the call of the seagulls.

Everything I did seemed to be what a good Christian should do, and I believed I was doing God's will, but something was not right. My life had no balance, and I had no idea how to change.

I remembered arriving home after that workshop. Family and work obligations quickly took over, and I reluctantly put the presenter's challenge and the graph on my "I-know-this-is-important-so-someday-I'll-do-something-about-this" list.

The journal rested in my lap, and the pen was poised between my fingers when the image of the dream popped back into my mind. Through this dream, God was again giving me insight about my healing journey. Something in me knew that the wall represented my life, and the ugly green paper represented the portion I had lived. The people pasting the squares were those who had put what they wanted on the wall of my life.

My mind wandered back to my childhood home where, from my earliest years, I knew I had no power. I grew up in a large family where those who had the power freely expressed their opinions and desires, while those without it were forced to ignore theirs. Through harsh experience I learned that the fewer desires and opinions I had, the less I was noticed and the safer I stayed. I also learned that to stay out of harm's way, I needed to just do what others wanted.

The lessons learned in childhood stayed with me. Cringing at the mental picture of that ugly green paper, I realized that I continued to believe I had little to no power. I ignored what I wanted and did what others wanted and expected of me. I went from one responsibility to the next, never feeling like I was doing enough. I even ignored reminders for medical appointments because I didn't believe I had enough time to fit them into my schedule.

When people asked what I wanted, I put the question to them and did what they wanted to ensure their happiness. To be honest, I rarely knew what I wanted because my life was focused on meeting other people's needs. I believed I was doing everything God was asking me to do, yet I knew God had given me this dream for a reason.

Opening my hands and lifting them off my journal, I prayed for wisdom. Proverbs 4:23 came to mind: "Guard your heart above all else, for it determines the course of your life." Ignoring my heart was not only my habit that had developed out of childhood trauma, but was something I had come to believe was God's will for me.

Though I memorized this verse as a child, I hadn't understood it as a command. As a result, I hadn't considered ignoring this command as disobedience to God. How had I missed this?

I often heard sermons about considering other people as more important than me, and I had been taught that to be a good Christian, I had to put others' needs above mine. Now I was facing a command that seemed the opposite of all I had believed was God's will for me, and one I had no idea how to obey.

I knew God's message through this dream was that He wanted me to take responsibility for what went on during the final one-third of the wall of my life. I also knew that to do that, I had to learn how to guard and care for my heart. Why did this command feel so daunting?

In my dream I wanted flowered wallpaper. I knew that if I wanted others to stop putting up ugly green squares, I would have to tell them to stop. My throat tightened and breathing became difficult when I pictured myself telling people I no longer wanted what they were putting on my wall. Saying I wanted to begin putting up flowered wallpaper instead seemed one of the most courageous things I could imagine doing.

I closed my journal and prayed. I asked God to heal this part of my heart that still feared upsetting people. I asked Him to give me courage to begin saying no to what I had been allowing others to put on the wall of my life. I asked Him to help me to remember that this verse was a command He was asking me to obey, and I asked Him to help me learn how to guard and care for my heart.

I put my journal away and began my day, but the dream has stayed with me, and God has answered my prayer.

God continued healing my heart. He helped me see that while sermons about considering others' needs as more important than mine are theologically correct, the enemy used them to keep me in bondage and to stop me from being who He was calling me to be. As I sought to honor God, He reminded me that He made me to live from my heart with the loves and desires He has placed within me. He reminded me that my heart holds the secret to who He is calling me to be, and what He is calling me to do with this one life I've been given.

When fears continued to haunt me, I pondered Proverbs 29:25, "Fearing people is a dangerous trap, but trusting the Lord means safety."

And when His command feels daunting, I remember James 4:17, "It is sin to know what you ought to do and then not do it." That verse helps me stay strong as I seek to live in obedience to God.

That picture of two-thirds of the wall of my life covered with ugly green squares of paper and the imagined picture of ending my life with the entire wall covered with that same paper have motivated me to continue seeking God's healing of my heart.

Much has changed in my life since I had this dream. At the end of that school year, I resigned. When asked to return the following year, I declined. I knew that was no longer God's will for me. I now spend time working to develop my skills. I am a published author, I speak for women's groups, and I lead retreats for women in my church.

I am still a responsible person, but God has shifted my areas of responsibility. He has helped me learn to pay attention to what my heart is drawn to. I take time to read for pleasure, and when my heart draws me there, I go to the beach.

Out of His great love for me, God gave me this dream so I could see what was plain to everyone but me. Out of His care for me, He is helping me learn how to guard and care for my heart.

I have not covered my dining room wall with flowered paper, but I regularly buy flowers for my dining room table. They remind me to say no to others' expectations that aren't a fit for my life, and to say yes to what brings me joy.

The Man in My Mirror

JEFF ADAMS

I couldn't look in the mirror. When I tried to, I didn't like what I saw.

I stood in front of the sink, hung my head, and wept. I needed to wash my face, erase my tears, and compose myself, since it was time to meet a friend for dinner.

But how can I face anyone when I can't even face myself?

Far from being the person I appeared to be at church—the person I allowed other people to see—I saw little in my life that had changed in the two decades since I had accepted God's forgiveness. I disguised the truth in an effort to hide my weaknesses and appear more spiritual. I prayed, but for the wrong reasons. I read my Bible, but more out of duty that became drudgery. I attended church regularly but felt little conviction and even less joy.

I believed I wasn't as good as the people I admired. But I did what I felt they expected me to do. I deceived myself and thought I fooled others. I lied to myself to avoid the pain of the truth about who I'd become.

I had wanted to be somebody—to do something great for God. So I became a pastor. My wife, Rosemary, and I considered our efforts a labor of love. We both worked jobs to pay our personal expenses. Every remaining waking hour we talked with neighbors. We led outreach teams from sister churches in other cities that passed out tens of thousands of flyers for special events. We organized concerts in nearby parks. We showed popular films. We hosted live performances of plays. We rented a small storefront building at a strategic intersection of two major roads. We held church services. I preached. We did everything we'd been trained to do. We drew sizable crowds to our events, but only a handful of people attended every weekend.

What am I doing wrong? What else can I do?

I'd forgotten that I could do nothing without God's help.

In time, a young man who won our confidence betrayed us. Our pastor and we had considered him to be faithful and trustworthy. In truth, he never stopped engaging in addictive and destructive habits. He stole the church's sound equipment, and with it, my hopes and dreams.

I listened to the lies my enemy screamed in my mind. *You didn't know what he would do. You didn't stop him. You were fooled. How can you help others when you couldn't help yourself?*

I echoed the accusations. *If I couldn't hear God warning me about this man, how can I teach others how to listen to God?*

We moved across town. We intended to start over. We never did. My attempt to build a congregation from scratch in a city where I knew almost no one grew from frustration to resentment.

The experience reminded me of the Wright brothers' flight at Kitty Hawk. Like theirs, our flight was short and bumpy with a rough landing. We limped away from the ordeal and moved to another city, too ashamed to go home to the friends and the church that invested so much in us.

I got a job. My wife worked. We fell into a comfortable routine. Go to church. Go to work. Eat. Sleep. And repeat the cycle. Weeks turned into months. I surrendered my dreams.

I gave up on God, but God never gave up on me.

Still, I doubted my abilities. Worse, I doubted my worth. We closed the church and I stopped pretending to be a pastor. I quit. *I failed. I disappointed God, my pastor, and our friends.* I saw myself as the young prodigal son in Luke 15. But I couldn't go home. *I've squandered everything.* Instead, we moved to another state.

I hoped to be of some use in another church, to serve a pastor we thought we knew. Maybe I could become his assistant. *That church is growing. They could use us.* That dream never came true.

Through a series of misunderstandings, a comment I made about the pastor became misconstrued: To prevent possible allegations of financial impropriety, I'd suggested a second signature be required on all checks over a small limit. The pastor thought I'd sown seeds of distrust among some of his leaders. Nothing I was accused of was true. That didn't matter. Someone inferred what I never implied. Gossip did the rest of the damage.

We left that church. Reluctantly, we moved back to Arizona.

I asked God why things happened as they did. *Why me? God, why didn't you help me? Why did others succeed and I failed?* I'd quit trying to answer those questions, but one more nagged me. *What now?*

I didn't know the answer. Instead, I tried to follow my pastor's advice. He urged me to ask, "God, what do you want me to learn from this?"

He cautioned me, "You need to learn to draw your dignity from the eternal, not the external."

He warned me, "You can come home, but I have nothing for you. No place. No position. No prospect of any ministry in the future."

People may have no use for us, but God always does. In time, Rosemary and I found ways to serve again. Yet we felt we were second-string players. We felt overlooked and tolerated at best, ignored and invisible at worst. I viewed myself as irrelevant and insignificant.

Years passed. Until that night in front of the mirror, I heard only silence.

In *The God Who Pursues* by Cecil Murphey, I'd read about a mythical beast, a basilisk. Part serpent, part rooster, according to legend, the hideous creature tormented and killed local villagers. No one knew how to rid the country of the ugly monster. Then someone realized the basilisk feared its own image. Repulsed by its reflection, the creature ran away.

The people gathered every mirror available. When the serpent appeared again, the townsfolk planned to surround their adversary and force it to stare at itself. The day came, and they seized the opportunity. Unable to escape, and compelled to look at its ugliness, the basilisk died of fright.

I felt like the basilisk. I wanted to slither away into the shadows where I felt most comfortable.

Unable to look up and face my reflection, I cried and prayed, *God, I'm sorry. How can you love me after what I've done? I disappointed my pastor and our church, but worse, I dis-*

appointed you. You've given me so much, and I have nothing to offer you.

I wanted to succeed to prove to God how much I loved Him. All these years later, instead of being the leader of a large congregation of committed people, I stood alone in a hotel room. I didn't want to face my past, and I was unwilling to face my future.

God, I've wasted everything you've given me.

I wiped the tears from my face and lifted my head. At that moment, I felt as if God stood behind me. We looked into the mirror together. He put His hand on my right shoulder and leaned close to whisper into my heart, "You should pray for that man in the mirror the way he prays for others."

I broke down again and sobbed. Then I thought about His words. I often prayed for others. I'd take their hands in mine, let them look into my eyes, and I'd say what they needed to hear most. *God's not mad at you. He loves you. He'll never stop loving you. And when you stumble, His grace will catch you.* My crying subsided.

God waited. Then He spoke again.

"You should speak to that man the way he speaks to others."

This time I didn't look away, although tears continued to stream down my cheeks.

I realized that God often prompted me to encourage others, to comfort them, to help them believe in themselves again. *You may not believe in you, but God does. He always has. And when you can't help yourself, He will come to your rescue.*

I relaxed, splashed cold water on my face, and blotted it dry with a towel. I stared once more at the man I barely knew.

God stepped closer and leaned against me. He wrapped His arm around my back, across both shoulders. Then He spoke one more sentence: "You should love that man the way he loves others—because I do."

I understood. I loved people, because God does. When I saw others unable to love themselves, I sometimes put my arm around their shoulders and whispered the answer to the question they couldn't ask—how can God love me? *Jesus doesn't love you because of what you do; He loves you because of what He did. Nothing you do or don't do can change that.* Oftentimes afterward I cried with them.

Now a small smile crept across my face. Tears of sorrow became tears of joy. I felt comforted by the peace God wrapped around me.

I love God because He loves me. I need to forgive myself the way I forgive others. I mouthed my gratitude in silence. *Thank you. I love you so much—because you love me.*

I brushed my hair and stood a little straighter and taller than I had in years. I looked at the man in my mirror. I didn't cringe at what I saw. Instead, I smiled again, grabbed my room key, and headed out the door to meet my friend.

I knew I wouldn't change overnight. But for the first time in more than ten years, my heart overflowed with hope. *I can be who God created me to be; my life can make a difference.* I faced the truth about myself: Failing didn't make me a failure.

He Can Open Any Door

ANNE PALMER

The wind-driven snow whipped the scarf from my head, and I dropped my keys. Struggling with groceries, I bent to retrieve the keys from the wet pavement.

I cannot let this get to me. I have been in situations most people wouldn't believe. This is temporary. The kids are being troopers. I will find a job soon. My résumé is in so many places, something has to break.

I fumbled with the retrieved key chain and blinked as the wind cut across my chapped cheeks. I pushed the key into the locked car door and turned it . . . nothing.

It can't be frozen. I was in the store less than an hour. Lord, you know how tired I am. I can't sleep for worrying about this job situation. I know you will work it out, but my bank account is almost empty. I have to get home, and now I can't even do that. Please open this door.

I looked to heaven and once more pleaded.

I put the key in the door again and *pop!* the lock opened. *Thank you, thank you, Lord.*

I slid the grocery bag to the passenger seat, got behind the wheel, and closed the door. An uneasy panic slowly brought chills to my spine. Unfamiliar candy wrappers were on the floor mats. The mats were different. *I am in the wrong car.*

I never moved so fast in my life. I don't know if I screamed as I bolted from that car, but all I could think was, *Why did you answer that prayer, Lord?*

My own car was on the other side of a large truck and was identical to the dark red Ford I had just trespassed into. *Phew.* I pulled out of that parking lot with sudden energy from the adrenaline rush and visions of accusations of auto theft.

My life had not been easy due to my own poor choices. Many years earlier I had married a man because he was good-looking. Jerod wasn't Christian, but I thought I could change that. He grew up in a home with parents who'd married because of an unplanned pregnancy. They openly hated each other, and Jerod was the battering ram they used to punish each other. He had never experienced love.

When I met him, he pretended to love me and to like everything I liked. I fell head over heels in love. I married him five months after we met. As my mother warned me, "Marry in haste, repent at leisure." Soon after I said "I do," I began repenting.

Not believing in divorce, I stayed and stayed and stayed. I had an aunt who was divorced, and she always seemed pathetic. She had no life of her own and was always with my grandparents. I was terrified of having a life like my aunt's.

Jerod was physically and mentally abusive. If Jerod had a bad day at work, he came home and took it out on me.

Once Jerod cornered me in the kitchen and slapped me over and over. I prayed, *Lord, please stop him, I can't take this.*

I clearly heard the Lord speak in my spirit, *Turn the other cheek.*

Is that you, Lord? I thought. But I did what He said.

I pointed to my other cheek and told Jerod, "Try this side for a while."

Jerod looked at me with shock, shook his head, and walked away.

Finally, sixteen years after our marriage, while I was attending a bridal shower for his relative, Jerod harassed our fourteen-year-old daughter, Laurie, treating her just as he had treated me for all those years. Our son, Luke, told me his father had grabbed Laurie's arm and screamed obscenities in her face.

This was intolerable. Laurie had not taken Jerod for better or worse. I had. I would not let her go through that kind of treatment. It was time to leave.

We packed clothes and left while Jerod was at work. We moved in with my father. We had lost my mother to a heart attack years before. My dad welcomed us, but the children hated their new school, and they had been through so much that I couldn't see them enduring any more.

Laurie told me she had nightmares of my returning to her father. So with my dad's help, I rented an apartment in the children's school district. I went to work at the local bank. The children were thrilled to be living in peace, and they began to enjoy a normal life.

From the time I was a little girl, I knew God heard and answered my prayers. Before I married Jerod, I knew the Lord had put many red flags in my path, which I ignored. That union was not God's will, but I really believed that if I showed Jerod love in a peaceful and loving home, he would be happy. I guess I had seen too many Hollywood movies.

God was always with me, through the abuse and through every angry word.

My most amazing experience happened after we left Jerod. Things had been quiet for some time. We were enjoying a peaceful existence, and I thought naïvely, *Maybe he is better off without us, too. He was never happy in our marriage.*

I let the children visit him, but I was afraid of going back to the house. I had rented a small U-Haul when we first rented the apartment, and while Jerod was at work, we retrieved a number of my dishes, pots and pans, and my son's twin bed. This enraged Jerod, but he was afraid of my father and couldn't come near us, not knowing exactly where we lived. He was treating Luke reasonably well, and the boy wanted to visit his friends near his dad's. I agreed.

At our apartment I was always careful when the doorbell rang. I screened people on the intercom before I buzzed them into the building. I thought nothing of it when the doorbell buzzed and Luke said, "It's me, Mom."

I immediately hit the buzzer so he could enter. A few minutes later I opened the door and there was Luke—and Jerod. Jerod pushed his way into the room before I could slam the door. Jerod immediately slapped me so hard I fell, hitting my temple on the tiled kitchen floor.

The children ran to their rooms as they always had, to escape the chaos. I was dazed but stood unsteadily as Jerod glared, his face just inches from mine. I felt a paralyzing awareness of Jerod drawing a pistol from his waistband. He backed me against the wall.

As he held me against the wall, he placed the gun inches from my forehead and said, "You are going to die." He screamed that I had someone else, and that I had turned his children against him.

Then I smelled the alcohol on his breath. Jerod never drank. He held the gun inches from my forehead. I immediately prayed, *Lord, you know I am not afraid to die, but if those children hear this, they will come running out and see the mess that was their mother and they will be traumatized for the rest of their lives.*

The barrel of the gun was right before my eyes. I could see every bullet in every chamber. It began to move slowly.

Suddenly it stopped.

I looked into Jerod's eyes. He looked confused, even shocked. He slowly lowered the gun to his side and walked toward the door.

I ran behind him, ready to slam and lock the door. He turned as he crossed the threshold and put his foot in the door to stop me. He glared at me and said, "The only reason you are alive is because God wouldn't give me the strength to pull the trigger."

As he finally turned and walked down the hallway, I slammed and locked the door. I slid to the floor, shaking so badly I could hardly retain a rational thought.

I struggled to stand, terrified he would return. Then relief flooded through me as I looked out the window and saw his car leave the parking lot. I thought about what he said at the door, realizing that God had indeed taken the strength from Jerod. That was the answer to my prayer and the only reason I was still alive.

Luke came out of the bedroom. "Are you all right, Mom? I am so sorry. Dad wouldn't let me tell you he was with me. He pulled me away from the speaker when I tried to tell you."

I hugged him and told him that it was all right, that there was nothing he could have done, and that we would go to my sister's house far away from here for a while. The relief on his face told me he was frightened, too. Tears welled in his eyes as he looked at the lump on my temple.

I phoned my sister. Nora had friends who were attorneys, and when I spoke to one of them, he advised me to see a divorce lawyer and stay at my sister's house until Jerod was served with a restraining order. Jerod was terrified of authority figures, so I knew he would not risk going to jail.

That was years ago. I know God answered prayers, one way or the other, but He does not do frivolous things. Why would He have opened that car door when it was the wrong car that winter day so many years ago?

I was feeling desperate then, since I was still out of work and unable to find anything. I had done everything I could think of and was pleading with the Lord to help me.

Shortly after that I received a call for the perfect job. I had applied for many, but this was the one I really wanted. God is good all the time.

My children are grown now and happily married. In those intervening years, the Lord took care of us every day, perhaps in less dramatic ways, but no less real. I met a Christian man who loves me and treats me as a husband should treat his wife. God is love. He has proven to me all my life that He is always with me. I am truly never alone.

A Pocket Full of Miracles

Laura Kingston

My idea of a miracle was set in stone—it comes as a bolt from the blue! A person is saved, healed, or changed in a heartbeat from whatever dilemma has befallen them. Divine intervention has made the impossible possible, the unchangeable changed, or the grieving joyful once again. Prayers are answered, usually in the nick of time, and fear and grief and tears are wiped away. The problem is resolved instantly, and the heart is so joyful that it feels as if it may burst.

At least that's what I thought. But perhaps, just perhaps, I was wrong.

I was a person who prayed diligently for a miracle that didn't come. I was someone who knew what my miracle needed to look like and accomplish—yet it didn't happen.

I searched my heart for what I had done wrong, wondering why God had not heard my plea and answered accordingly.

So why had God not answered? Well, He had answered. I just didn't know it.

In 2009, the business my husband and I ran, like many others, began to fail. So much was going on at the time, and I knew we should sell it, but my husband thought the economy would come back and the business would return to its former productivity. It didn't.

My husband's health hit a snag; my dear father, who lived seven hundred miles away, was struggling with heart failure; and the business continued to spiral downward. I felt like a millstone was around my neck and I was drowning. And I couldn't find my faith.

My father passed away. After we had made the final arrangements and said our good-byes, life continued. My mother needed to come and live with us. There was a house to sell and pack, and a new living space to prepare.

But there were blessings. My mother's church friends helped pack. We could never have done it without them; they were a little miracle I had not recognized.

The business continued its death spiral. We sold it for one-third of what we had paid for it. At least we were out from under it, but we still had a very large debt to pay, and bankruptcy was not an option.

The thought of losing my home terrified me. I began to awaken in the middle of the night with a jolt; it felt as if I were suffocating. I would take a huge gulp of air and ask, *How? How are we going to survive our financial dilemma? How are we going to pay the bills? How are we going to get by? How are we going to avoid being bankrupt? How? How?*

I missed my dad, and I missed the financial security the business had always provided. My heart and soul were raw and oh so painful.

Then came the miracle. I didn't recognize it as such, and I almost missed it. One night, with my usual awakening, a voice in my head said, "Don't ask *how*, ask *what*. *What* do you need?"

My miracle was just a single word: *What!*

"Okay," I said. "What I need is some financial relief. What I need is to stop worrying about every penny. What I need is a job. But how can that happen? Who is going to hire a woman my age?"

Oddly enough, the next day I walked into my favorite antique mall, struck up a conversation with the store manager, and asked if they were hiring. "Yes," she said. "When can you start?"

One week later I was working as a stager at the antique mall, and my husband found a job, too. The pay wasn't great, but it was enough, and I was thankful. Not a bolt from the blue, but just a little relief and a bit of faith renewed.

With every problem—and some were bigger than others—I prayed for what I needed, not how it would be resolved, and each prayer came with a little miracle. I prayed, *What do I need to forgive?* not *How can I forgive?* and forgiveness came. I prayed, *What do I need to find peace?* not *How can I find peace?* and my new church provided it.

They did not all come at once, but they came, just little miracles, one by one, until one day I realized I had a pocket full of miracles.

If I had been hit by that bolt from the blue, would I have been as grateful? Would I have seen the resolve? Would I have known that God, in fact, does work in mysterious ways? That He did, that He had, in fact, answered my prayers?

I am ashamed at my lack of faith. But He renewed my faith.

Actually, the failure of the business was a blessing. Had that not occurred, I would not have my foot on a new path. My heart is so joyful it may burst!

God always answers our prayers, and a miracle is a miracle no matter if it is big or small. So just step aside and don't ask Him *how* He is going to do it, just tell Him what you need and let Him figure out the details. Have faith and trust in Him because He knows what you need and He loves you! And that is the greatest miracle of all.

Swan Song

SANDRA MCGARRITY

I opened the Sunday church bulletin and a brochure fell out. I picked it up, curious to see what it was. I scanned the heading and inwardly groaned. *Oh, just another Wednesday evening class for women.*

My attitude wasn't because I had something against women's classes—I would recommend them to anyone. I just didn't want to go to one.

Nevertheless, I sighed and read on. The title caught my eye: *Living Beyond Yourselves.* It sounded sort of interesting. It would probably be fun to share a class with other women. It could be life changing. The Lord probably wanted me to go. He was probably definitely telling me to go. I could probably go. But I didn't want to go.

So the battle began. I tried to forget about the class, but the idea of it kept coming back to mind. I mentioned it to different friends but couldn't seem to make a commitment. I had some long, stern talks with myself.

You should really go.

I have very good reasons to not go.

If you don't go, you will rob yourself of a blessing.

If I go, I will probably have a disaster of some sort.

Et cetera.

Absolute panic took over. I prayed and prayed some more. I was still in a panic.

You see, I have a disability. I'd had the neuromuscular disease for most of my life but had worked hard to overcome it. I'd made it through four surgeries and the accompanying hospital and rehab time, and extended time out of school. I'd shed the leg braces I'd worn for ten years as a child. I had become almost "normal" as a teenager.

I had married, given birth to and reared two daughters, and had a career. I was a true overcomer. Then, in my early forties, the physical condition began to go downhill again.

At first it was just weakness in my lower legs. Then, climbing stairs became more difficult. I adjusted and didn't mention it to anyone except my husband. Within a few years, I was having serious trouble propelling myself forward and being able to keep balance at the same time. I knew I needed help, but I didn't want help. I just wanted life to be the way it had been.

Then, one night, I had to stop every few minutes to regain balance on the walk into a class at church. I was alone and realized I had barely made it inside without falling. I was taking a real chance on an injury.

The next morning, I knew the day had arrived. I drove to the local pharmacy and chose a sturdy cane. It helped my balance so much, I should have felt happy. Instead, I felt as if I were giving up. I felt cheated and wondered why I had worked so hard just to go back. I felt old.

In time, my physical condition grew worse until the day we went to the medical supply for a walker or "rollator," as they called it. I felt that a walker by any other name still stinks. But it was just for "distance walking," so I could still go to the mall and similar places, since the cane was no longer enough.

I was grateful for the freedom the walker gave, but I was making another adjustment that felt like a trek on the downward path. It wasn't long before the walker morphed into a device for short-distance walking and was replaced by a wheelchair for distances.

So, here was the rub about the class.

My husband worked nights and couldn't take me. I wouldn't be able to use his arm for one side and my cane for the other as I did on Sunday mornings. No one at church had ever seen me with the walker.

Oh, how I hated that walker. My mind equated it with being an old lady, and I wasn't old. Yes, it was a pride thing, but it was a pride thing I was seriously struggling to give over to the Lord. Let's face it; needing help is often portrayed as something humorous in our world. Movies, commercials, and TV shows poke fun at elderly people with walkers.

Worse than that, we are told we can overcome anything if we only try hard enough. Now, there were certain things I would never be able to do no matter how hard I tried, but using the walker always made me feel I wasn't trying hard enough. It was a symbol of personal weakness, or worse, as many thought, a lack of faith.

Finally Wednesday afternoon came, and I got in the car to drive to church. By this time the Lord had done a lot to calm me, but nerves were still trying to get the better of me. On the way there I was thinking about elderly people and how they look with their walkers, trying to convince myself that anyone could tell I wasn't elderly, and maybe I didn't look so bad.

Still not knowing why I cared so much what I looked like, but knowing I did, I prayed a strange prayer. "Lord, let me see a younger person with a walker. I need to see what they look like to the observer just to reassure myself."

I truly expected the Lord to give me the sign I asked for since it was what I thought I needed. All the way to church I kept my eyes peeled for my young person with a walker. Surely, he or she was just around the next corner. When I arrived at the church driveway without seeing my sign, I chuckled.

"Okay, Lord, I knew it was a silly request."

I drove to the back of the church, since the elevator was near there. I parked, switched off the ignition, and began to gather my things. My hands trembled in spite of my efforts to keep calm. I still dreaded going in with the walker.

A large pond sat directly behind the back parking lot. My car faced this pond. Just as I looked up, ready to get out and get the hated walker, I saw something I had never before seen on the pond. A majestic white swan with her head held ever so gracefully glided past. When it was directly in front of my car, it turned its head and bestowed a regal look upon me. I looked on as it tucked its head close to one wing and swam on by.

We had often seen fish jumping from the water. We had seen many types of birds and even an owl around the pond, but we had never seen a swan there. Yet a huge, snowy white swan paddled in front of my eyes. I sat transfixed, unable to look away.

"How beautiful," I breathed.

At that moment, God spoke to me in a voice I heard deep in my heart.

That is exactly what you look like to me when you use the walker.

"No," I whispered. "That can't be."

But I knew it could be and it was. I broke into tears as I was reminded I am beautiful in His sight because He loves me. God sees that a person trying to do His will, no matter how stumbling, is beautiful in His sight. Only God has perfect vision to see beyond what man sees. God looks on the heart.

I took a last look at the swan, got the walker from the back seat, held my head high, and glided into that class. Of course, everything worked out fine. No one looked at me strangely or questioned me in any way. I didn't feel at all bad about myself. I just felt amazed inside by what the Lord had shown me.

The next day, I told my husband about what had happened. The following Sunday we scanned the pond for a glimpse of my visitor, but it was nowhere in sight. The next week and any other time we were at the church, our eyes automatically went to the pond. We didn't see that swan or any swan on the pond again.

So many times since that day some years ago, I have used the memory of the swan to get past some hurdle—imagined or real. I've been reminded more than once that no matter how I felt or no matter how someone else perceived me, I could lift my head and go on. My God sees me as I had seen the swan—beautiful in His sight. It reminds me of the story by Hans Christian Andersen:

> But what did he see in the clear stream below? His own image; no longer a dark, gray bird, ugly and disagreeable to look at, but a graceful and beautiful swan. To be born in a duck's nest,

in a farmyard, is of no consequence to a bird, if it is hatched from a swan's egg. He now felt glad at having suffered sorrow and trouble, because it enabled him to enjoy so much better all the pleasure and happiness around him.

The Ugly Duckling by Hans Christian Andersen

When Miracles
Come Full Circle

JEANETTE GARDNER LITTLETON

S hould we cancel the well visit this morning since Teresa's coming to town?" I asked my husband, Mark, that October morning.

Our son had been born ten days earlier—actually, on my birthday, and was overdue for the well-baby visit he was supposed to have within his first week. But with my getting used to being a new mom, the visits from family, and the busy director of Christian education job my husband and I shared at a nearby church, I'd been in a fog and was slow to schedule him to see the family doctor.

And now Teresa was coming to town. Teresa was a dear friend from my hometown, Kansas City, fifteen hundred miles away, where I'd lived until I'd married my husband and moved to

Maryland slightly more than a year earlier. We only had a short window of time with Teresa. She'd been at a conference on the Chesapeake Bay, and her ride was going to drop her off at our house for a few hours. Then we would take her to the airport.

I'd been terribly lonely in this new city; it was so different from home. And when I married Mark, I'd instantly become a full-time stepmom to the six- and thirteen-year-old daughters he had custody of. A new city, new marriage, new family, new job . . . I only had one new friend nearby and really missed my support system back in Kansas City. I was really looking forward to seeing my friend's familiar face and hearing the news from home. I was looking forward to a good, long chat.

"Maybe we're trying to fit too much into the day," I said. "Teresa will be here for such a short time. And after we take her to the airport we have to be back before the girls get home. I wish I knew the way to the airport so I could just take her myself. Maybe we should just reschedule the visit for another day. After all, it's just a well-baby appointment. It's not like he's sick or anything."

I was already exhausted from the night feedings and all the other things that come with a new baby. I really didn't want to go sit and wait in a doctor's office, and by the time we got back, I might be too tired to really enjoy Teresa's visit . . . and focusing on her was definitely my priority for the day.

"Well, whatever you think," Mark replied. "It would probably be okay to put off the doctor's appointment."

Gardner grinned at me and squirmed. He was more responsive than I expected a newborn to be.

"Yes, you're already a smart, healthy little cookie," I cooed. "Daddy's probably right. I'd much rather take you in when things aren't so hectic. I think we should reschedule for next week."

But for some reason I just couldn't pick up the phone. It would certainly make life easier . . . but something inside me just didn't feel right, something indiscernible and persistent would not let me cancel.

"Oh, let's go ahead and go. We should be home in plenty of time before Teresa gets here," I determined.

Before long I bundled up Gardner in his Winnie the Pooh outdoor onesie that dwarfed his tiny body. Mark carried him in his scratch-free, brand-new car carrier to our burgundy Toyota and carefully hooked the seat belt.

At the doctor's office, Gardner started crying. By the time the physician tried to place her stethoscope on his chest, he was screaming, his whole tiny body stretched out red and stiff as he hollered.

Try as I might, I couldn't calm him down.

"Maybe he's hungry," I suggested, feeling like an idiot for not being able to calm my infant. The physician left us alone in the room while I tried to nurse him. He didn't seem very hungry, but then, so far, he hadn't been a big eater at all.

Finally the doctor tried to take her stethoscope to his tiny chest again. Her eyebrows furrowed.

"His heart rate seems high," she said. "Perhaps it's because he was crying so much. Let's try it again in a few minutes."

But in a few minutes, and then again a few minutes after that, her frown deepened as she kept listening to his chest.

I wasn't really picking up on her concern. I'd seldom been in a doctor's office in my life and, at that stage, didn't know how to read the clues.

"Let me go check something," she said.

I looked at my watch in concern. We needed to start thinking about getting home since it was about time for Teresa to be dropped off there. Maybe Mark should go back to the house? But then he'd have to come back and get Gardner and me. No, surely we wouldn't be at the doctor's much longer.

She strode back into the room. "There's a pediatrician's office downstairs. Dr. Wendell McKay. I've checked, and he can see you right away, so I'm going to send you downstairs. He's more used to infants and needs to take a look at Gardner."

"Oh. Okay," I said as I grabbed the diaper bag, puzzled about what was going on. "But we have someone who's supposed to be at our house in a few minutes. . . ."

"You really need to see Dr. McKay first," the doctor firmly said.

Down in Dr. McKay's office, the baby and I were quickly swept into an exam room while Mark lingered to give insurance information.

I'd never met Dr. McKay, but as he straightened up from examining Gardner, even I realized that his kind, brown eyes looked concerned, and maybe even a bit alarmed.

"Your son's heart is beating fast . . . much too fast," he said.

"He was crying pretty hard earlier," I commented.

"No, it's more than that," he gently explained. "He needs to go to the hospital. But not the local hospital. They're not set up to deal with infants who have these symptoms. You need to take him in to Johns Hopkins in Baltimore."

I still wasn't getting it. "But can it wait? We are late in meeting a friend at our house. She's probably waiting for us there now."

"Well, yes, you need to get there without dawdling," he said. "Go to the ER. We'll let them know you're coming."

The words *emergency room* seemed to break through my fog. If the pediatrician was sending us to the ER, well, they were obviously concerned about something. I looked at Gardner.

His tiny white body was barely any bigger than the doctor's large, dark hands. He seemed as mellow as he'd been most of the time during his short life. I figured we'd get to the hospital and they'd tell us everything was fine.

Johns Hopkins was thirty minutes north of us, right up the highway. And thankfully, the airport was on the way. We could pick up Teresa from our house and drop her off at the airport on our way to Johns Hopkins. I calmly made the plans, still not really understanding the urgency of the situation.

Teresa was sitting on our front step when I approached her. "I hoped this was the right place," she said, laughing.

"I'm so sorry we're late. We were at the doctor's office for the baby's well visit," I explained. "And I'm not sure why, but they're telling us we need to go to the hospital—not the local one, but the one in Baltimore."

"Is Gardner okay?" Teresa asked, her eyes wide open.

"I'm sure he's fine," I said. "But I don't think we'll be able to take you for lunch. I'm sorry, but I think we'll have to drop you off at the airport. I know it's a while before your plane leaves, so I'm sorry . . ."

Teresa waved aside our apologies and filled me in on my friends back home while we drove to the airport. She jumped out of the car with, "I hope Gardner's okay. I'll be praying!" and on we went.

At Johns Hopkins we were ushered right in to a fairly large emergency room cubicle and were instantly surrounded by people and instruments. Mercifully, I don't remember much about the experience except for praying silently and being unnaturally calm.

As healthcare workers checked his heart and hooked machines up to him, Gardner started crying again, and he really picked up the pace when they tried to put needles into his little arms for an IV. I held him and gently tried to soothe him. Repeated IV attempts failed, so they finally placed him in a bassinet under a heating lamp and worked to find a vein in his head where they could poke the needle successfully. I still held on to his little body, quietly comforting Gardner and asking God to be with my baby.

"I can't believe you're a first-time mother," one of the nurses said. "We don't usually let moms in while we do this because they get hysterical."

Before long, Gardner was sent to NICU, where he was wrapped like a little burrito with only his head popping out of the blanket. Mark had gone home to take care of the girls, so I sat in the rocker by the bed alone, trying to absorb everything.

"Your son's heart is going well over three hundred beats per minute," the pediatric cardiologist eventually explained. "Normal for a baby is one hundred to 150 beats. We are giving him some medications to try to slow his heart down."

I learned that my son had SVT, Supraventricular Tachycardia. For some reason, his heart was not pumping blood through the chambers normally. Instead, the heart rhythm was off, causing the heart to beat fast in the upper chambers until it finally kicked into the proper rhythm again.

Within the next few days, the medical team in the NICU finally found the right combination of medications that brought my son's heart rate down. I was surprised to find that three times a day he'd be taking one medication and twice a day he'd be taking another—and I recognized both of the medication names as ones my father was on for his heart.

"Will he have this condition the rest of his life?" I asked at another consultation with the doctor.

"It might be that his heart just hadn't quite finished developing," the doctor said. "We'll send him home with medications and he'll come in pretty frequently for EKGs right now. He may grow out of it entirely and be able to be off the medication eventually. But regardless, it's a good thing you brought him in when you did."

"Really? It's life-threatening?" I asked.

"Mrs. Littleton, with the rate your son's heart was beating, he would not have lasted much longer. Maybe a few hours, but certainly not even twenty-four hours."

The doctor went on to his other tasks, but I sat in the rocker, stunned.

I think we should reschedule for next week.

The memory of my words made me shudder as my mind superimposed the doctor's "He would not have lasted much longer" over them.

I had seriously come so close to cancelling that visit. And if I had, my son probably would have gone into cardiac arrest and not survived. My own heart still beats fast when I think about that call I almost made—and how God saved my son by keeping me away from that phone and pushing me reluctantly to the physician's office. I consider that nothing less than a miracle.

Before he was two years old, after medication and monthly EKGs, the pediatric cardiologist proclaimed Gardner free from the symptoms of SVT. He didn't know if Gardner's heart had just matured into beating properly or if there was an electrical issue at play.

"If he is going to have it later in life, the symptoms might flare up in his teens, as his hormones change," he explained. "And by then, he'll be able to tell you if something is going on with his heart."

Gardner's elementary years passed uneventfully as our healthy, active son kept busy.

In middle school, Gardner's drama teacher gushed about his abilities. "He really is gifted," she told us. "I think he could easily get a scholarship in drama."

His high school teacher seemed to feel the same way as he gave Gardner four separate speaking parts in the school play and signed Gardner up to participate in competitions with dramatic and comedic monologues.

But one day Gardner came down the stairs from his bedroom saying, "Mom, I want to tell you something."

Gardner had always known about his babyhood experience with SVT; I'd always mentioned it on his school and camp health forms—that he was to be taken seriously if he complained of his chest feeling odd. And now he confessed that his heart had been beating hard and fast. It was starting to scare him.

"Gardner, how long has this been going on?" I asked.

"It started about nine months ago," he said. "I was just trying to make my heart calm down by making myself relax, and it worked for a while. But now, anytime I get nervous, like when I do drama stuff, I can't control it."

We talked with the cardiologist's assistant at the office where my husband normally went for his heart issues. She grimly scolded Gardner for trying to self-medicate and proceeded to schedule tests. One great coincidence was that the cardiologist who specialized in the electrical circuits of the heart and worked with children and teens had actually been Gardner's small-group leader at church during his middle school years. So we were assigned to Dr. Chapman, someone Gardner already felt comfortable with.

"We can do one of two things," Dr. Chapman said when the test results were back. "We can give Gardner medication that should help regulate his heart. Or we can do an ablation. The electric circuit in Gardner's heart is messed up. But the problem appears to be in an easy place to get to. For an ablation, we would go into his heart through his wrist or his loin, just as we do for a heart catheterization, and we would basically fry the spot where the problem is. That would probably cure his SVT for the rest of his life."

I frowned. By then, my husband had undergone several heart caths and stents. I didn't know if I could handle my son going through a similar potentially life-threatening procedure.

Oh, God, I wish you would just do a miracle and heal his heart! I cried silently.

But aloud I asked, "What do you recommend, Dr. Chapman?"

"I recommend that we do whatever Gardner decides he's ready for," Dr. Chapman said. "He's seventeen and is a level-headed young man."

"Gard?" I asked, turning to him.

"I want to try the meds first," he said. So once again, my son started regularly taking some of the same heart medication his grandfather had taken, and that his father now took for heart issues.

Despite the medication, Gardner's heart still raced. His racing heart before medication had terrified him, and now, even with medication, the stress of competition still pushed his heart to racing, so Gardner ended his drama career during his junior year of high school. The cardiologist increased his dose several times as the SVT episodes continued. And I continued to silently pray that God would work a miracle in my son's life and heal his heart.

Finally, Gardner came to me with weariness in his voice. "Mom, I just want all of this to be over with."

He was ready for the surgery.

The ablation was scheduled for just before our birthdays during his senior year. A lot had changed since my first trip to the hospital with Gardner. This time I was more seasoned, after going through many hospital procedures with Gardner's dad, grandfather, and grandmother.

But this time I also understood the severity. As we entered the hospital that morning, I wished I was as naïve and foggy as that young mom had been nearly eighteen years earlier.

This time my husband sat with me in that waiting room that was so familiar to me—the cardiac waiting room where I'd prayed and figuratively wrung my hands a bit while my father and husband went through heart procedures.

Finally we were called into consultation with Dr. Chapman. The ablation had been a casebook success. Gardner's heart was beating strong and normally. It was cured. They would keep him overnight for observation but expected no complications.

That night my son and I watched TV and joked around in his hospital room as I created a makeshift bed on the vinyl couch.

"I love you, Gard," I said as I started to turn off the light. As I looked at his smile, I realized the miracle had come full circle. The first miracle was when we were at the doctor's office just at the right time for Gardner's SVT to be caught and his life saved. That, I feel, was a supernatural miracle. And now, the second miracle was the surgeon's ability to take a tiny instrument through the veins into my son's heart and completely cure the problem.

Sometimes ministers skilled in praying lay hands on ailing people, and God heals them. This time, a godly man skilled in surgery placed his hands on my son, and God healed him. And that's a miracle, too.

Prayer Paths to Healing

ROSE MAUREEN

Prayer has always been a double-edged sword for me. I have never had a problem praying for others enthusiastically, and I can usually manage to pray for myself. But when I ask anyone else to pray for me, it gets complicated. I don't like to bother them or have them nag God on my behalf, so I either pretend that everything is fine or say "unspoken" when asked for a prayer request.

I was not raised in any sort of religious environment, and things got much worse when my dad died. After his death, my mother went from being a lapsed Catholic to an angry atheist who forbade me to ever speak of spiritual things.

After my high school graduation I chose to follow the teachings of Jesus. When my mom died of an overdose a few years later, my faith did not waver; instead, my spiritual relationship matured. Even as I felt sure of my relationship with the Lord, I kept my relationships with fellow Christians at a distance. I suppose I was suffering from some sort of low self-esteem when it came to interacting in prayer.

One day shortly after I relocated to a new state to be closer to my adult children who were attending college, I woke up with extreme pain in nearly every area of my body. After a series of tests, I was diagnosed with sarcoidosis. Sarcoidosis is a chronic disease in which lymphocytes, a type of blood cell, become overactive. These overactive lymphocytes release chemical substances that cause granulomas (a collection of inflammatory cells) in various organs of the body. In most cases, the disease appears only briefly and disappears on its own. In 10 percent of patients, the disease is chronic.

I was at the most serious level with sarcoids in my lungs, liver, spleen, skin, lymph glands, bones, joints, and nervous system. I was given an extremely high dose of steroids to make sure that no granulomas lodged in my brain or heart, since sarcoidosis can cause death if the disease causes damage to these vital organs.

I was told the chronic use of steroids results in many well-known side effects, including weakened bones, fluid retention, high blood pressure, mood swings, and confusion. Less well known is that they can also cause eye problems.

After several months of steroid use, I began experiencing eye problems. My optometrist sent me to an ophthalmologist, who prescribed ophthalmic solution drops for my steroid-induced glaucoma. The small bottle cost nearly two hundred dollars and was not covered by my insurance.

I had to purchase the drops, since not treating glaucoma can lead to blindness. I was taken off the steroids to avoid any further damage and began going to the gym to rid myself of the excessive weight the steroids had caused.

One day while I was leaving the gym, I realized my gym bag had been opened and some items had been removed. I was upset but not that worried because I thought I'd had only a small amount of change, a pack of gum, and my spare keys in a pouch. When I got home and was ready to take the eye drops, I realized the thief had also taken those.

I called the pharmacy, but they could not give me a free refill. I called the eye clinic, but they would not refill the drops until I came in and got rechecked because my eye doctor had recently retired. Then they called me back to tell me my new insurance would not cover any part of the visit so I would have to pay more than four hundred dollars to see the specialist and get the drops.

In a panic I went to the emergency room, and they referred me to another ophthalmologist. The doctor was in a teaching hospital, and I had to wait another seven days for an appointment. I was afraid of seeing a doctor I didn't know and getting more bad news, so I started to pray. But for the first time in my life, I found that I could not pray.

The fact that I went blank when trying to pray scared me as much as the thought of going to the eye doctor.

On Monday morning, a week before my appointment, I went to a Bible study. Just seven of us were there, and the study dealt with preparing for Advent. George, a lively seventy-something who still played jazz piano at swing clubs, asked if anyone had a prayer request.

I was going to say "unspoken" as I had always done before, but that word would not come out of my mouth. I quickly explained about my lost drops and my future eye appointment.

George and the others prayed for me. George promised to pray for me the rest of the week and mentioned a verse he had read.

On Tuesday I went with my friend Joyce to a women's-only breakfast and Bible study on the book of John. Before the study was over, there was a time for praise and prayer requests. At this point, thinking about my eyes was making me ill, so I vowed not to mention it at all, especially since everyone else seemed to have praise reports.

The lady sitting next to me smiled and gently nudged me. "I am sure there is something you need to pray about. . . ." she coaxed.

I explained about my eyes, and she laid hands on me and prayed for a miracle. Then she opened her well-worn Bible and told me to write down a verse.

On Wednesday afternoon I learned my friend Clayton had the flu. Clayton is a tough ex-Marine, an advocate for the homeless, and someone who never misses a shift serving in our local soup kitchen. I knew if he missed volunteering he must really be ill, so I decided to call him. As soon as he said hello, he explained that he had been praying for me. He was not sure why, but he felt he needed to. He began to pray, and then he gave me a few verses that he felt led to share.

On Thursday night some neighbors were having a potluck and a Bible study. They were going through the entire book of Psalms line by line, and I usually enjoy this study. But I was so tense I didn't catch much of the teachings.

As I was leaving, my friend Dave said he wanted to speak with me. Dave is a prayer warrior who is never without his Bible and his prayer journal. He said he had noticed I was quiet, so he felt it was important to pray with me.

Whenever he had made such a request before, I would make a joke and leave or just say "unspoken," but I felt his sincerity, so I told him about my eyes. He wrote down my need and prayed for me. Later he mailed me a note with some verses on it.

On Friday I went to my friend Kathy's fellowship meeting. On this night there was a guest teacher—a man who was part of her church's healing ministry. Kathy had told him about the sarcoidosis in my lungs, so I thought that was what he was going to pray about for me. Instead, he prayed about my eyes. Later, as I was leaving, he handed me a brochure with information about church events, and on the top was a verse.

The following Monday I went to the new eye doctor, where I had a diagnostic exam that consisted of mini tests. In one test I was asked to look straight ahead while indicating when a moving light passed my peripheral vision.

After that, eye drops were used to numb my eyes and contact lenses were placed in them. These lenses had a mirror that showed the doctor if the angle between the iris and cornea was closed and blocked (a sign of glaucoma). Then he did an ophthalmoscopy: He used a small device with a light on the end to illumine and magnify my optic nerve. If the intraocular pressure was not within the normal range or if the optic nerve looked unusual, that was another way to reveal if a person has glaucoma.

None of the tests showed any sign of glaucoma, and the scarring I had from past infections was gone.

The ophthalmologist could not explain why my eyes showed no disease when two other doctors had said I had eye disease and I'd spent thousands of dollars during the past fourteen months to treat it. The drops I had been taking never claimed to cure glaucoma, only to keep it from getting worse.

This ophthalmologist sent me to get another opinion with an eye doctor who works with eyes with sarcoidosis. The second doctor also found no trace of glaucoma.

He said there must have been a mistake with the original tests. I told the doctor what George, Rebecca, Clayton, David, and Kathy's friend told me—even though they had never met each other or known what the others were praying. They all shared with me that same verse: "Jesus looked at them intently and said, 'Humanly speaking, it is impossible, but with God everything is possible'" (Matthew 19:26).

To God be the glory.

About the Contributors

Jeff Adams is a pastor, teacher, and speaker. He lives in Arizona with his wife and daughter. He's not afraid of mirrors and enjoys helping others see what God sees.

Jan Apilado has been married for forty-six years and is blessed with four children and eight grandchildren. She loves to sing, write, and tend her organic garden.

Mary L. Ball is a multi-published author and member of American Christian Fiction Writers. She resides in North Carolina and enjoys singing with her husband at church functions.

Swanee Ballman is a retired book editor. She and her new husband are active in their church. They enjoy grandparenting and traveling.

James Stuart Bell is the owner of Whitestone Communications, a literary development agency, and the compiler of seven volumes in this inspirational story series.

Veronique Bennett writes from her home in Syracuse, New York.

Molly Noble Bull, www.mollynoblebull.com, writes novels. *Gatehaven*, her Christian Gothic novel, won the grand prize in the 2013 Creation House fiction-writing contest in the historical category.

Emma Chambers is a writer living in the southeast with her husband of forty-one years. She is blessed with two daughters and a granddaughter.

Vicki Davidson's ministry goal is to provide encouragement for life in a complicated world through her writings and presentations. She has a master's degree from Calvary Theological Seminary.

Sharon Rene Dick is a legal assistant and Sunday school teacher. She has written for *The Kids' Ark* magazine and *Splickety Love*.

Susan Eryk and her husband live in Florida with their three children and grandchildren nearby. She loves to write and babysit, but seldom simultaneously.

Dianne Fraser lives in Busselton, Western Australia, with her husband, Neil, and two sons, Jayden and Callum. She is a graduate of Perth Bible College and works at Cornerstone Christian College.

Nanette Friend is a writer and a speaker. She has contributed to *Stories of Faith and Courage from Prison* and is co-founder of Set Free in Him Ministries. Contact her at nfriend06@yahoo.com.

Elizabeth Garrett is a writer and editor and owns a web-based marketing services company for authors. She also serves as team leader for Bartlett Christian Writers in Bartlett, Tennessee.

Sharilynn Hunt is the founder of New Creation Realities Ministry, Inc., www.ncrministry.com. She is the author of *Prevailing Prayer.*

Jeanie Jacobson is author of *Fast Fixes for the Christian Pack-Rat* and enjoys writing *Chicken Soup for the Soul* stories. Connect with her at www.jeaniejacobson.com.

Roberta Kautz is a freelance writer. She speaks for Stonecroft Ministries and is a guest speaker for Christian women's groups. She and her husband live in the Bay Area.

Laura Kingston, a member of the Ozark Highlands Christian Church, is pursuing a new career as a Christian life coach focusing on women over fifty.

Jeanette Gardner Littleton is a writer and editor living in Kansas City. She co-directs Heart of America Writers Network (www. HACWN.org) with her husband, Mark.

Julie Ann London is passionate about sharing God's love and His Word with those needing encouragement and hope.

Rose Maureen is a writer from Monrovia, California.

Sandra McGarrity lives and writes in Chesapeake, Virginia. Her writing has been published in many books and publications.

Julie Miller is a certified spiritual director and the owner of Heart Matters Publishing Company. She and her husband, Rey, live in White Bear Lake, Minnesota.

Kelly Wilson Mize is a wife, mother, and school librarian in Huntsville, Alabama. She writes books, curriculum, and hundreds of devotions and articles.

Anne Palmer lives in California. She has written two novels and leads an evangelistic outreach.

Trish Propson is a speaker, author, columnist, and multi-generational relationship advocate. Meet Trish at www.cornerstone comm.org.

Marty Prudhomme has written and taught Bible studies for twenty-five years and is a freelance writer and speaker from Louisiana. Contact her at marty770@bellsouth.net.

Rita A. Schulte is a professional counselor. She is the host of *Heartline Radio* and *Consider This* on 90.5 FM in North Carolina. Follow her at www.ritaschulte.com.

Ingrid Shelton is a retired teacher and librarian, and a freelance writer. She is an avid gardener and loves to walk and visit shut-ins.

Dayle Allen Shockley is an award-winning writer and a writing instructor in Houston. Her articles and essays have appeared in dozens of publications.

Carol Nash Smith is a retired English and journalism teacher living in Hot Springs, Arkansas, with her science-teacher husband. She loves to read, watch birds, travel, write, and cook.

Richard Spillman is the founder of the Kingdom is Near Ministries and the author of *Do What Jesus Did*.

Patti Ann Thompson traveled in ministry, singing and sharing God's Word for more than twenty-five years. She desires to help women discover the "you-nique" way God made them to fulfill His purpose. Learn more at www.pattiannthompson.com.

Roberta Updegraff is an author with Guideposts Books. She enjoys volunteering in a Honduran orphanage, traveling, reading, quilting, and researching genealogy.

Susan M. Watkins, award-winning author, wrote for *The 700 Club*. She's featured on CBN.com. Additional partnerships include Gloria Gaynor and Max Lucado.

Michelle J. Welcome is a speaker, copywriter, and author. Her books include *Spiritual Diseases of the Unbridled Tongue* and *Overcome Secret Sins in 15 Days*.

Karen Wingate directs women's ministry activities and several Bible studies. Her blog appears at www.graceonparade.com. She and her husband live in western Illinois.

James Stuart Bell is a Christian publishing veteran and the owner of Whitestone Communications, a literary development agency. He is the editor of many story collections, including *Angels, Miracles, and Heavenly Encounters*; *Jesus Talked to Me Today*; and *Gifts From Heaven*, as well as the coauthor of numerous books in the COMPLETE IDIOT'S GUIDE series. He has cover credit on more than one hundred books, and he and his wife live in a western suburb of Chicago.

More True Stories of God's Love and Provision

Compiled by James Stuart Bell

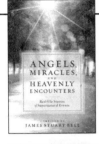

This fascinating look at the supernatural world offers more than forty true stories of miraculous provision, encounters with angels and demons, near-death experiences, and incredible rescues. You'll marvel at how God and His angels are working behind the scenes to protect and guide us.

Angels, Miracles, and Heavenly Encounters

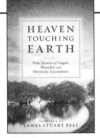

Miracles, healing, divine provision and protection—this compilation of true, uplifting stories will touch your heart, strengthen your faith, and remind you that, even when it seems God isn't at work in your life, there is a loving Father who is always working on your behalf.

Heaven Touching Earth

In this inspiring collection, people who have seen Jesus, heard His voice, or experienced His miraculous intervention share their amazing stories. You'll find hope and encouragement in these accounts of Jesus' ongoing intervention in the lives of believers like you.

Encountering Jesus

BETHANYHOUSE

Stay up to date on your favorite books and authors with our free e-newsletters. Sign up today at bethanyhouse.com.

Find us on Facebook. facebook.com/BHPnonfiction

Follow us on Twitter. @bethany_house